This page is intentionally left blank.

Stefan Bruvelis

Social Class and Caste: A Study of Ethnicity in Colonial Latvia and Race in America

Published by: Kindle Direct Publishing

Text Design by: Ana Costa

Cover Design by: Ana Costa

A CIP record for this book is available from the Library of Congress Cataloging-in-Publication Data

ISBN-13: 979-8-9863039-1-8

Contact the author at Stefan.bruvelis@gmail.com

Stefan Bruvelis

SOCIAL CLASS AND CASTE: A STUDY OF ETHNICITY IN COLONIAL LATVIA AND RACE IN AMERICA

Publisher

to Emily + Matt

to a new self awareness
of our heritage!

Stefan Bruvelis

[signature] 10/15/22

Social Class and Caste: A Study of Ethnicity in Colonial Latvia and Race in America

STEFAN BRUVELIS

Acknowledgements

To the lives that the United States has sentenced to imprisonment or generational poverty because of the color of their skin. For if I had carried on with the hooliganism of my teenage years, including all of my encounters with law enforcement, except with dark skin, I wouldn't be alive to have written this book.

To Cale Seis and Eryn Carlson, a teacher and a journalist, for your foundational input to the book's structure at both the macro- and micro- levels.

To everyone else who took the time to read rough drafts (or just listen to me) and gave the confidence to not write this project off as a dream.
And thank you to Noe Morales, my spouse and best friend, for guiding and supporting me to becoming a better person these weeks and months I've been writing.

Introduction

A map of Latvia created by this author using a blank template borrowed from Wikimedia Commons.

This book is about Latvia, a country I trace my heritage and identity to. Before continuing with my main arguments, however, it is worth a little introduction to this country for the unfamiliar. Latvia is a country in northeastern Europe the size of West Virginia and with under 2 million inhabitants. The countryside is mostly flat and boggy, but it can also have areas of elevation no higher than a few hundred meters above sea level. Latvia is heavily forested with boreal species such as spruces and pines, although there can also be birch and alder. The Daugava River bisects the country, and Latvia generates most of its electricity from hydroelectric power there.

Latvia is between 56° and 58° latitude north, comparable with northern Quebec or Juneau, Alaska. This results in twenty hours of light in summers, and equally long nights in winter. The country is south of Estonia, but it is further north than Germany, France, or Ukraine. The country's long coastline faces the Baltic Sea across from Sweden, while to Latvia's east are Russia and Belarus.

The sea significantly moderates Latvia's climate for being so far north. Dairy, fish, and pork form a significant portion of the diet, but Latvia also produces lots of timber, berries, and rye or buckwheat. Valuable mineral resources, besides amber, are scarce. The largest city, by far, is the capital, Riga; the country's next largest city, Daugavpils, has just 15% of Riga's population. Most of Latvia's population is ethnically Latvian and speaks the Latvian language, but there are significant Russian minorities in all of Latvia's urban areas since Soviet times.

Latvia was an independent state from 1918-1940, after which the Soviet Union illegally occupied it for fifty years. Since becoming independent again in the 1990s, Latvia has become a member of both NATO and the European Union. Latvia has three major historical provinces; from west to east they are Kurzeme, Vidzeme, and Latgale. While Kurzeme and Vidzeme are historically Lutheran through Baltic German influence, Latgale is historically Catholic through Polish influence.

Chronology of Latvian History

18th Century Latvian Chronology

1700—1721: The Great Northern War ends Sweden's hegemony of the Baltic and Russian control begins.

1710: Riga capitulates to Tsar Peter.

1710—1711: The Great Plague kills 2/3 of Livonia province's population as well bringing about the extinction of the Livonian language in eastern Latvia.

1712: The Russian "plow-share review" redistributes land and total indiscretion to local German barons over the lives of the indigenous Latvian and Estonian peasants. Functionally, the peasants become property of the landowners.

1712—1740: Economic and social recovery from war. Corvee becomes inhumanely heavy. Foundation of "half-estates" which function as colonial plantations that profit their owners. Vodka production accelerates and peasants sink into alcoholism.

1737: The Moravian Church explodes in popularity amongst peasants as it encourages education and literacy while threatening the aristocracy's authority.

1739: The Declaration of Baron Rozen distorts history by establishing a myth of centuries of Latvian enslavement.

1743: The Moravian Church is banned in Russia for its perceived threats to the social hierarchy.

1750s: Paster Eizen is the first Baltic German to publish writings aimed at reforming indentured servitude in Latvia and Estonia.

1762: Catherine the Great repeals the ban on the Moravian Church.

1765: The first official patent by the Baltic nobility encourages improvements to the status of indentured peasants.

1771: Unrest in Livonia and armed revolt by peasants after the patent is side-stepped.

1772: The first partition of Poland (Latgale, north and east Belarus are incorporated into Russia).

1784: The Poll Tax uprisings erupt in Livonia.

1789: The French Revolution's storming of the Bastille inspires Latvian and Estonian revolts again.

1793: The Second Partition of Poland (Ukraine east of the Dnieper, Minsk are incorporated into Russia).

1794: The Kosciusko Uprising seeks to expel Russian influence from the remnants of the Polish Commonwealth.

1795: The Third Partition of Poland (punitive for Kosciusko's Uprising) erases Poland and Lithuania from the map.

1796: Russia begins to conscript young Latvians and Estonians for life sentences in the army. Baltic nobles use this to threaten, intimidate, and punish rebellious or disobedient peasants.

19th Century Latvian Chronology

1802: The peasant uprising at Kauguri frightens Baltic German nobles enough to finally undertake modest reforms.

1804: The first reform project of Livonia is drafted to give the Latvian peasant private property.

1807: Napoleon's "freedom of the birds" arrives for Polish serfs, giving them personal freedom but no ownership of land.

1812: The defeat of Napoleon erases the threat of meaningful reform in the Baltic.

1809–1823: The Great Land Survey of Livonia (Mērnieku Laiki) assesses private property meant for Latvian peasants.

1816–1819: The Great Land Survey is ignored, and while serfdom is officially repealed in the Russian Baltic provinces, all the land remains the nobility's private property. Laborers are only nominally free to choose their place of employment.

1819–1820: Unrest in Courland province and outside Riga to protest this theft of peasant land.

1830: Another Polish uprising leads to increased Russification and forced conversion to Orthodoxy across Russia.

1836: The Petrograd/Warsaw railway is completed, leading to increased integration with the Russian Empire.

1841: The Warm Lands Movement begins. After its failure, punitive expeditions are launched against peasants in Jaunbebri and Pühajärve to discourage further emigration and labor shortages.

1840s: Latvian peasants convert in mass to Russian Orthodoxy to protest the Lutheran Church, which upholds noble interests.

1850s: In Livonia, despite thirty years passing since serfdom's official repeal, 82% of peasants still pay rent with their labor rather than cash.

1857—1863: The medieval walls of Riga are torn down to expand the city, accommodate its growing population, and allowing industrialization.

1861: Serfdom is repealed across the Russian Empire.

1862—1865: The publication of Pēterburgas Avīzes challenges Baltic German supremacy in print for the first time.

1860s: On federal orders, Baltic German estates are divided and sold to Latvian peasants in century term mortgages.

1880s: The liberal Tsar Aleksandr I is killed by a bomb; his successor Aleksandr III reinstitutes Russification and repression as well as support for conservatism and traditional, feudal values.

1890s: The New Wave (Jaunā Strāva) movement of young Latvians embrace socialism and labor strikes in opposition to this conservatism.

1896: Mass emigration of Latvian peasants, already popular since serfdom's abolition, increases as the Trans-Siberian Railway opens.

1904: The unpopular Russo-Japanese War leads to widespread labor strikes.

1905: The Revolution of 1905 consumes the Russian Empire, but especially in urban and non-ethnic Russian areas.

1906: The tsar agrees to establish a representative government and parliament as a concession for the 1905 Revolution.

1913: Riga becomes the top export port in the entire Russian Empire.

1914: World War I begins, interrupting Latvia's complete Russification.

World War I Chronology

1914 (Summer, Fall): Latvians are mobilized in the Russian army for World War One. They are sent to East Prussia, where the Germans slaughter them, the first of many Russian military blunders.

1915 (Spring, Summer): Germany invades western Latvia, stabilizing the front along the Daugava River. Meanwhile, the Russian government pursues a scorched earthy policy, emptying western Latvia of its inhabitants.

1915 (August): The Latvian Riflemen begin accepting volunteers.

1916-17 (Winter): The "Christmas Battles" and the 'blizzard of souls' result in so many deaths amongst Latvians that they undermine further Latvian support for the tsar.

1917 (March): The tsar is overthrown, and Latvian Riflemen are radicalized by communists and Social Democrats.

1917 (September): The German army captures Riga.

1917 (November): The Bolshevik coup overthrows the interim Russian government. Communist leadership in eastern Latvia begins a terror.

1918 (March): The Germans force the Russians to accept the Treaty of Brest-Litovsk, with penalties and concessions far harsher than those imposed on Germany after World War One.

1918 (April): German prepares to colonize Latvia with ethnic Germans.

1918: Many nations in eastern Europe declare independence, including Ukraine, Lithuania, Poland, Estonia, Belarus, and Finland. Latvia alone delays.

1918 (November): Germany signs a truce with the Entente on November 11, ending World War I; Latvians proclaim independence on November 18.

1918 (December): The Bolsheviks return to the Baltic to reincorporate the territory into the Soviet Union. They force the interim Latvian government to shelter on the battleship Saratov.

1919 (April): Baltic German nobles and other conservatives recapture western Latvia and Riga from the Bolsheviks. The Estonian army halts any further German advance in June.

1919 (October): The warlord Avalov Bermont leads his pro-monarchist "West Russian Volunteer Army" to attack Riga and overthrow the Latvian government once and for all.

1919 (November): The Latvian national army liberates Riga on 11 November (one year to the day after Armistice Day) and drives Bermont's army from the country.

1919-1920 (Winter): With the help of Poland, the Latvian army drives the Bolsheviks out of eastern Latvia. The government nationalizes all estates formerly belonging to Baltic Germans and begins redistributing them to landless peasants.

1919-1922: The Latvian Agrarian Reform dismantles Baltic German supremacy forever.

Kur tie krievi, kur tie krievi?" As a 7-year-old on my first trip to Latvia in 1999, my howls pierced the gabled rooftops of Old Town Riga, the Latvian capital. The country had been independent from the Soviet occupation for only eight years now, but for me, born in 1992, that was quite literally a lifetime. "Where's the Russians! Let me at them!"

A few pigeons rustled their wings as I tore across St. Peter's church steeple, hunting for these so-called occupiers. A young, cigarette-smoking couple on the balcony apparently understood enough of my Latvian to exchange amused glances, extinguish their cigarettes, and shuffle toward the elevator. These were local Russian-speakers, who in 1999 composed 59% of Riga's population and 43% of Latvia's as a whole. This was the legacy of four decades of Soviet colonization.

While nobody in my family encouraged the rants, my fixation on the 'undesirable' demographics of the country of my grandparents was rooted in my earliest lessons. Since toddlerhood, I'd learned all about the Communist tanks of 1940 rolling into their once prosperous, independent, and Latvian Riga. My grandparents also shared stories about family members being deported to Siberian concentration camps in cattle cars. These childhood life-lessons always highlighted the hypocrisies and monstrosities of Godless communism, coupled with a strong dose of Catholic doctrine. However, it was I who latched onto vocalizing my hatred for the demographic legacy of Russian colonization, never them.

Before World War II, Latvians of the First Republic composed 75% of the population, and for the first time in seven centuries of foreign domination, the Latvian language had official status. Once the Soviet Union illegally occupied the Baltic states in 1940, however,

Russians and other Soviet citizens flooded the socialist republic for factory jobs and leadership roles in the new planned economy. In Riga, as in many other parts of Latvia, it became entirely possible to live one's life not speaking a word of Latvian; the proletariat 'liberated' from bourgeois nationalism were expected to bow before Moscow's demands. The situation was most acute in 1989, just preceding the Soviet Union's collapse, when ethnic Latvians composed only 52% of the whole country's population and were the minority in all of Latvia's seven largest cities.

On Christmas Day of 1999, months after my cousins, father and I had returned home to the United States from our Latvian vacation, I anxiously watched my cousins play *Medal of Honor* on the PlayStation. "Kill those Russians!" I shouted. "Show no mercy! They don't belong in Latvia- someone just needs to wipe them all out!"

"Stefan," Cousin Dan said, setting aside his 90's era controller after raiding the video game's bunker, "your great grandma was a Russian, you know that right?"

That Christmas, after I'd hollered enough vitriol to rouse the dog on the floor from a doze, I experienced my first case of cognitive dissonance. I experienced my first exposure to the knowledge that 'good' and 'bad' people are not simply divided by their language or parentage, but by their choices. After all, if my blood suddenly contained one-eighth of the 'occupier,' did I too deserve to die then?

After I returned home, my father explained to me that his grandmother, Marija Podzņakova, was from Moscow, and had married Fēliks Brūvelis, a Latvian. To honor their mixed heritage, the couple named their two children Gunārs and Igors. My grandfather, Igors, got the Russian name, which earned him endless taunts from his Latvian aunts, who mocked "Iggy" even after his father abandoned the family. Nonetheless, despite their ethnicities, Marija spoke fluent Latvian and Fēliks spoke Russian, a fact my father demonstrated with their love letters from the 1920's, which he'd photocopied and archived.

Ten years later, in 2008, as an octopus-like 15-year-old (intelligent, reclusive, and awkward), I rode on a coach bus with 20 other Latvian American teens during our first "heritage tour" of Latvia without parents. I was at a tremendous disadvantage here; not only did all the other participants recognize one another from "Garezers," the Latvian summer camp in Michigan, but they all spoke better Latvian than I did. After all, I'd only began to seriously study the language at age 14, with my conversations limited to the reports I had to write on assignment before the tour.

As our bus hurtled down a rainy two-lane toward Cape Kolka, the conversation drifted to what games we'd play at the next naktsmāja, likely an old Baltic German noble's manor refurbished as a bed and breakfast. Momentarily emboldened, I gambled on the most random and ridiculous thing a teenager could think of: "Iesim krievus medīt! Let's go hunt some Russians!"

"Krievus medīt!" The boys of the group guffawed, but I knew I'd crossed the line when a chaperone raised her voice menacingly. She waved me to another row, where I took a seat and stared at the vibrating carpet of the bus to receive my lecture. "Krievi ir cilvēki tāpat kā latvieši – Russians are people too, and we do not hunt people for fun, or even joke about it." This was a lesson sorely learned: before World War II, some 100,000 Jewish people lived in Latvia. In 2008, an identical number of Jewish graves and memorials had replaced that total.

In June of 2014, at age 21, I returned to Riga for my third midnight sun there while on a mission trip with my Latvian Lutheran Church. By the time of this trip, my machine-gun syllables of Latvian slang had irritated my Americanized mom so much that she'd scrunch her face and demand I slow down or repeat myself in English. I took pride in how far I'd progressed my command of Latvian. It was also on this trip that I first learned the Latvians living in Latvia never even considered me one of them.

"He's from America and he's trying to practice his Latvian!" My cousin Jānis exhibited me like a rare primate to a group of boys on the tram at Krišjāņa Valdemāra Street in Riga. Throughout the Baltic squall that afternoon, we'd ridden the line to the beach and back, me posing questions in Latvian and Jānis replying in the enthusiastic British English he'd picked up working abroad. Our spectators had been fascinated enough by this collision of East and West that they'd remained on the tram an extra two stops to catch the finale.

"Well, I guess you are somehow, in some way Latvian," another cousin, Oskars, wrote to me on Instagram as we formulated plans to bury a great-uncle's ashes I'd brought along in my suitcase from America. After both of these instances in 2014, I experienced the same cognitive dissonance as when I'd been rebuked years earlier for shouting that all Russians ought to be annihilated. So, I wasn't even Latvian after all, either?

In the United States, because of my name ("Steffen Bru-something"), classmates growing up always viewed me with a mix of curiosity and hesitation, appearing just like one of them but not quite fully. As an adult, I have learned this is a common experience for descendants of immigrants still displaying anything foreign about them in the United States. Taking my own light complexion and European features for granted, I did not accept until 2020 that this could still sometimes be a matter of life-or-death in the United States.

Given my anti-communist inoculations from an early age, I recognized that history could also be written to tell myths, untruths, and outright lies. The first example I remember learning as a child was the sham-referendum of 1940, during which the USSR arranged to 'consensually' welcome the bouquet-waving Baltic States into the communist paradise (albeit at gunpoint and amidst a military occupation). With this perspective, I saw the portraits-on-parade of Stalin and Lenin as equivalently evil to those of Hitler, perhaps even more so, for they are still displayed with fanfare in Russia today despite their crimes. It wasn't until 2020 that I accepted this phenomenon of historical amnesia pervades the United States, my home, as well.

In November of 2014, after I'd returned from Europe, news reports from Cleveland, Ohio circulated that the police had shot unarmed 12-year-old Tamir Rice, just months after similar riots erupted in Ferguson, Missouri for another police shooting of an unarmed black man. Safely nestled in the Minnesota suburbs that November, cultured from my summer in Berlin with döner kebab, roundabouts, and the U-Bahn, I bristled at this disorderly American behavior. Perhaps if the black men who'd been shot had just complied with orders, things wouldn't have gone so out of hand? Meanwhile, Facebook memes contrasted the orderly queues of light-skinned Japanese who'd survived a tsunami in 2011 with dark-skinned looters; I didn't want to hear anything about skin color not accounting for differences!

Ruminating and giving form to my media-stoked aggression, I posted my own hot-take on Facebook, a phenomenon that would only snowball that autumn and become one I would regret for years. What did these Black Lives Matter (BLM) performances have to prove other than causing chaos for families trying to make their holiday season merry and bright? Couldn't black people divert their energy toward minding the gangs, investing their money, and addressing the black-on-black violence *nobody* ever talks about? How many ambulance rides had failed due to protesters obstructing the highways? Why did all of BLM's actions seem just like another invitation to hate them?

Fully aware of the Soviet Union's lies and imperialism, nonetheless, I was still infected and gullible to another empire's lies since birth— the lies and traditions of the United States. I was complaining about disrupted Christmas shopping but ignoring that American police can still literally lynch unarmed black Americans at traffic stops. I cannot solely blame the education system for this ignorance – after all, my social studies teachers encouraged our investigation and discourse regarding the Indian removals of the 1830s, the brutalities of Jim Crow, and so on… no, instead I was infected by white supremacy, and had been for my entire life.

With smarmy outbursts like something from Milo Yiannopoulos's playbook, I pulled up a podium to the Table of Oppression as a "gay Baltic American" and issued one Facebook memorandum after another. I ladled up buckets from my experience as a Latvian American, urging black Americans to draw from our common tradition of musicality and historical enslavement– to hold another Singing Revolution like the Estonians did in 1989. Never mind that I ignored the American justice system exonerating the men who lynched Emmet Till in 1955, or that American sheriffs, lawmakers, and authorities today are still very often Klansmen (Dearen, 2021). Instead, I plugged my ears and kept jabbering about how in 1989, two million Latvians, Lithuanians, and Estonians had joined hands in a human chain to literally sing their rejection of the Soviet occupation. "Looting and burning only delegitimizes a movement," I insisted; Latvians were superior to black Americans, I implied.

The greatest lie I ever told myself, repeated since childhood to exonerate myself of the guilt all white Americans share in maintaining America's caste system, was that I had nothing to do with it. My family came to the United States in the 1950s, fleeing the colliding locomotives of Stalin and Hitler, well after slavery or the Confederacy. My burgeoning white fragility meant I became infuriated anytime I saw the hashtag #checkyourprivilege, which I nursed into vile and arrogant paragraphs on Facebook. Instead of studying black American history, I chose to vocally stand for white supremacy, without ever using that term of course.

While in 2016, I'd been horrified and publicly vocal against a compromised, pro-Russian president taking office, I also remained secretly satisfied that Donald Trump was a slap in the face to outspoken black Americans everywhere. In contrast to Latvians in the Soviet Union as late as the 1990s, my white supremacist doctrine told me that after the civil rights movement, black people had nothing to be ungrateful for in the United States anymore. Now that the playing field was finally 'level,' if black Americans would only curtail their self-destructive tendencies, then, like the Latvians of the early 20th century, their progress could be truly unstoppable.

A visit to the Latvian Church of Minneapolis in 2019 changed this thinking. Behind the glass cabinet doors of the church library, I descried an 11-volume series there titled "Daugavas Apgāda Latvijas Vēsture" (DALV)– a history of Latvia written in 1000-page, century installments. Already from the first volume I opened (1500—1600), the quantitative tables and analysis refuted nearly every conclusion I'd made about Latvian history until that point. The DALV series undermined the supremacy I afforded Latvian culture over 'less industrious,' 'less resourceful' peoples. For instance, from reading about the 18th and 19th centuries, I learned that I descend from Latvian peasants who burned and looted private property for 150 years in the name of seeking equal rights –and far more aggressively than black Americans in Minneapolis did after George Floyd's murder.

Whereas I once felt threatened by black rage and black self-defense, in 2020, I learned that as a Latvian, I descend from peasants who burned and looted private property frequently and ferociously. Through revolts nearly every decade from the 1700s to 1920, successive generations of Latvians protested Baltic German supremacy, and the exclusion of Latvians from property ownership, by using both violence and mass-emigration to cause labor shortages. Certainly, this will trouble many conservative Latvian Americans committed to 'law and order,' overturning our notion of superiority to 'disorderly' black Americans. However, I also hope it provokes a reckoning with what the United States affords a person based on their skin color— yes, especially in the racist North.

In 2020, I also read the two most important works of American history I've ever encountered: the Warmth of Other Suns and Caste, both by Isabel Wilkerson. These books provoked my third instance of cognitive dissonance when they toppled my conception of the United States as being any more righteous than the Soviet Union. I learned, for instance, that in the 1950's, Lithuanian and Polish war refugees looted, pillaged, and terrorized black Americans for trying to escape the South Side of Chicago and integrate into white neighborhoods like Cicero, Illinois (Wilkerson, 2010, pg. 373-74, 388-89). From these books, I learned that white housewives in the North made their black maids eat their lunches from dog bowls on the floor (Wilkerson, 2010, pg. 334) and that that Detroit factories hired Southern black migrants solely as strikebreakers (Wilkerson, 2010, pg. 275). From these two books, I realized that despite my Latvian heritage, I am just as culpable in upholding Northern racism as if my family came here when Americans still owned slaves.

This book is not a Black or Native history of the United States, and it does not intend to speak for black or native voices. Instead, this work challenges the mythologized history of Latvia celebrated today with an original analysis when relating to current social events in the United States. For a more authoritative explanation of Black or Native history, I recommend the books 1491: New Revelations of the Americas Before Columbus by Charles C. Mann, The Warmth of Other Suns by Isabel Wilkerson, and Caste: The Origin of Our Discontents by that same author.

As Wilkerson wrote in Caste, for me and so many other Americans, 2020 truly was the year of perfect vision.

With the buck-toothed smile of a 9-year-old, I tore open the envelope containing the invitation to a classmate's swimming-pool birthday party in 2001. The pool at Shoreview Community Center, where the party would be held, had it all – waterslides, floating animals, hot tubs. Nonetheless, its greatest feature there was surely the 30-foot, floating python.

On the day of the party, the water veritably boiled with fourth graders vying to climb aboard this serpent and dislodge one other from its slippery back. From a distance to the other partygoers, I too wrapped my arms around the snake but flailed, too weak and overweight to get a leg up. Nonetheless, determined to keep trying, I gasped for air as muscles I'd never needed on land suddenly throbbed for oxygen.

Just then, another swimmer jostled the snake, and I slipped off, tumbling underwater. Chlorinated pool water rushed up my nose, while a splitting headache sent me sputtering back to the surface. The other swimmer grinned down at me from the snake as he offered me a shockingly blanched, waterlogged palm, one in direct defiance of his black-skinned forearms. My skin crawled viewing his coarse, twisted worms of African hair peeking out of his scalp.

At that moment, a tingling and inexplicable disgust replaced the shock of flooded sinuses. I realized the water "tainted" by this coarse-haired, black-skinned boy had also probably infiltrated my nose, practically burning my brain! I reacted as if the serpent had transformed into a living, twisting python in front of us. I splashed and thrashed away from the snake, climbing out of the pool, and purifying myself of the black 'pollution' in the hot tub.

I recall this shameful anecdote of childhood racism only to illustrate the degree to which white supremacy permeates children, yes, even in "progressive" Minnesota. Despite my ostensibly "non-racist" upbringing, the unwritten rules of American society still instructed me from childhood that black people are somehow "untouchable" and "polluted"- certainly without wording it this way. My anecdote from 2001 is proof that amidst my 'post-racial' upbringing, my behavior wasn't some Technicolor relic from the 1950's, but rather, integral still to upholding the racial hierarchies here. These racist preferences infect not only children, but also adults, be they police officers, employers, lenders, judges, or members of Congress.[1]

All throughout my childhood, between my non-American name and my energetic Latvian analogies, other classmates considered me eccentric, certainly the "least-American" among them. Simultaneously, I remained incognizant of the pressures to assimilate that my own uncles experienced in the 1950s when they arrived as children from German refugee camps.[2]

Because of how other children always viewed me differently, and because my parents raised me in a bilingual environment with weekly exposure to Latvian at Saturday school, I often considered myself more "Latvian" than American. But by reading The Warmth

---

1. Latvians will widely agree that Russians found colonization of Soviet Latvia so attractive because they could find good jobs according to their ethnicity, not their merit or competence. If we can all agree that employers in Soviet Latvia prioritized hiring Russians over indigenous Latvians, then why would we ever deny the black voices saying racist hiring practices still underlie American society? Why would we ever rail against affirmative action?

2. My mother once described her brothers' childhood pressures to assimilate. She said that when it was time to come home from play, my Grandma Tekla called out to Uncle Aleks "Sandri nāc!" (Sandrs, come!) and to Uncle Leopold "Poldi, ūūū!" (Leopold, hey you!) The neighborhood boys, hearing this, thereafter nicknamed my uncles "Sandy Nuts" and "Poldy Lou". The only people crueler than adults, my mother summarized, are children.

of Other Suns and Caste, I learned that my knee-jerk racism at the Shoreview swimming pool in 2001 was perhaps the most American thing about me. Author Isabel Wilkerson depicts how in the 1950s, a swimming pool in Youngstown, Ohio made the white members of a local Little League team exit the pool so a black teammate could be floated for a few laps in a raft, instructed to never touch the water to avoid 'polluting' it (Wilkerson, 2020, pg. 120). With this attitude so pervasive across the Midwest at the time, black American children rarely learned how to swim, nor could their impoverished and redlined neighborhoods likely afford to maintain community swimming pools. Thus, the stereotype that black people "can't swim" has nothing to do with "bone density" or "too many crocodiles" in Africa but is an entirely Northern creation.

As I grew older, I honed my skills at hiding my unease around black bodies, cloaking myself in a sage robe of "non-racism" to avoid the issue altogether. Since childhood, I'd already tried inoculating myself against racism due to my heritage. Not knowing, at that time, about the 1950s racial crimes by Lithuanian immigrants against black Americans in Cicero, Illinois, I reckoned that my family had nothing to do with Jim Crow, segregation, or burning crosses. I even reckoned that maybe it was for the better if everyone just tried 'moving on' from racism. At the cusp of age 15, hoping to carve out a more 'Latvian' identity for myself and be exonerated from America's sins, I dipped my toes deeper into the blended myth and facts of Latvian history.

During that summer of 2007, I consumed reams of Latvian folk and choral music through my first-generation iPod after formally learning the Latvian language's highly inflected grammar. This 'dainu skapis' ('poetry cabinet') was composed independently by thousands of serfs using the only possession the Baltic Germans, legal owners of the land, couldn't strip from them- their voices. Among the songs included in canon Latvian national repertoire, Gaismas Pils depicts an independent, pre-Christian Latvia as a mythical castle of light. The sampled lyrics below were foundational to my conception of Latvian history:

> *"A bloody sun dawned over the Fatherland – "The nation was enslaved as heroes fell in battle.*

> *"Our stately Castle of Light quickly sank and disappeared."*

> *("Asiņainas dienas ausa Tēvuzemes ielejās; Vergu valgā tauta nāca, Nāvē krita varoņi;*

> *Ātri grima, ātri zuda, gaismas kalna staltā pils")*

Thus, through classic works of Latvian poetry, by age 15, I came to believe that a period of enslavement was canon to our national history. As an American teenager also grappling with the racial legacy of the United States, it was inevitable I would link my heritage to the black Americans around me. I noticed that whatever the Latvian composed threshing linen under the baron's whip, the black American composed on the plantation into Gospel spirituals. Music was a form of passive resistance everywhere.

Beyond Gaismas Pils, however, perhaps no other line of text shaped my impression of Latvian history than this: "Here, people are cheaper than negroes in America" ("Šeit cilvēki ir lētāki kā nēģeri Amerikā"). After interpreting the poetic works of Latvian identity, I devoured Uldis Ģērmanis' Experiences of the Latvian nation ("Latviešu Tautas Piedzīvojumi,") a textbook published for teenagers of the Latvian diaspora. Ģērmanis attributes the quote to an 18th century pastor, August Wilhelm Hupel (Ģērmanis, 1990, pg. 157), though it matters less who said it than how it resounded with me. My stomach churned as I pictured blue-eyed, blonde-haired Latvians wearing the same sackcloth as black slaves, occupying the same hovels as a people I subconsciously knew to be "the lowest of the low."

Despite the Latvian and black American common traditions of musicality amid enslavement, with which I could have empathized for my dark-skinned classmates, instead I used Hupel's quote to cling to my whiteness. It wasn't my fault, I reasoned, that durag wearing classmates got suspended for fighting in class (see 'school to prison pipeline'), or that black girls were the loudest and crassest in the room. How did their parents expect them to advance as professionals with first names like "Marijuana Pepsi?"[3]

Instead of recognizing that white America continues to criminalize being black, I ignored one successive police shooting after another. Instead of siding with the black American, with whom Latvians share common themes of oppression and musicality, I continued to plug my ears and permit white supremacy to blotch my heritage and reality.

Likely conceived of some white fragility toward a 2007 racial headline (and probably still a little insulted at my heritage being 'cheaper' than a black slave), I initiated a mental 'pissing contest' between Latvians and black Americans. My artifice involved taking the total time of American chattel slavery as 244 years (1619-1863), adding that to the period until civil rights ended racism 'once and for all,' and concluding with 345 years of black American oppression.

---

3. Names, like songs and voices, are another possession that cannot be taken from someone when everything else has been taken.

In contrast, I marked the year German missionaries founded Riga in 1201 as the beginning of 'foreign domination,' equated this with "chattel slavery" (which it was not) and concluded the period of political dependence only with a declared Latvian statehood in 1918.

With math and logic more problematic than a Confederate Army monument in Washington, D.C., I calculated that Latvians had survived 717 years of oppression, twice that of black Americans! Never mind that I cherry-picked my facts, entirely disregarding a century of "Good Swedish Times" (Labie Zviedru Laiki) from 1629- 1710, when generations of Latvians and Estonians enjoyed immense protections under the Swedish crown. By my logic, my ancestors had suffered for 372 years MORE than black Americans, while emerging from it with their heads held high, their own nation-state, and even speaking their original language. So long as I ignored that black Americans were kidnapped and stripped of their identities when being trafficked to America, it became easy to wonder what inhibited black Americans if not some innate primitivity?

Instead of recognizing that black Americans are "guilty until proven innocent" in America, or that three quarters of white Americans own their homes while 60% of black Americans rent, I entrenched myself in my own racist convictions. In 2020, however, after reading the DALV series of Latvian history and the Warmth of Other Suns, I finally realized that I had only accepted my conclusions because I depended on mythologized Latvian and American histories. Before 2020, I believed that glorious Latvian chieftains had ruled from wooden hillforts until the first German missionaries interrupted our natural greatness. Before 2020, I accepted my racist conclusions about black Americans because I truly didn't know the extent of Northern redlining and their exclusion from private property.

When the Minneapolis police murdered George Floyd over an alleged counterfeit 20-dollar bill in 2020, I finally accepted that the civil rights movement did not dismantle white supremacy in America, but merely buried it. As we see from one viral video of police harassing or killing black Americans after the next, "deniable racism" pervades this country. After all, it is much harder to sympathize with someone deemed a "criminal," "felon" or one "complicit" in their own misfortunes, than with someone hanging from a tree.

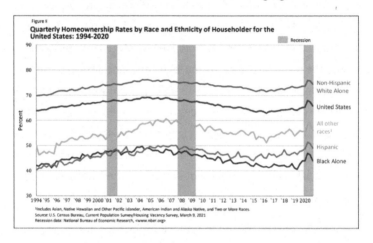

Quarterly Homeownership Rates by Race and Ethnicity of Householder for the United States: 1994-2021. A chart taken from the 2020 U.S. Census data.

As I learned from the Warmth of Other Suns and Caste, because of the Great Migration from the Southern U.S. in the 20th century, black Americans were restricted to Midwestern ghettos like Chicago's South Side or the Cabrini Green. White families, meanwhile, escaped to the suburbs. Starting in the 1930s, the Federal Housing Administration classified areas already occupied by black Americans in the North as too "hazardous" to lend to ("redlined" them). After World War II, the G.I. Bill also denied its returning, black servicemen the same low-cost, low-interest mortgages that it afforded white soldiers, furthering the racial gaps we see today. As a result, poor neighborhoods became poorer, the racial discrepancies in the North were solidified.

Crammed into tenements and working long hours away from home, black parents lost their children to inner-city gangs. In the 1980s, President Ronald Reagan sentenced generations of black Americans to further poverty by criminalizing the victims of the crack epidemic in his "War on Drugs." Rather than rehabilitating those black Americans as white opiate addicts are today, Reagan stripped these "felons" of their voting rights. Ronald Reagan's legacy and "criminal records" thus continue sentencing many black Americans to generational poverty.

Today, white Americans must take responsibility for the condition of the "blighted" inner-cities and ghettos, for they are exclusively the product of white American racism. Of course, the Republican Party conveniently blames Democrats and black Americans for this modern segregation. This historical amnesia is analogous to the Soviet Union's cover-ups and gaslighting regarding its own tremendous crimes.

Until white America addresses its role in creating and upholding the inner-city ghetto in the 20th century, in excluding black Americans from generational wealth, then America's "freedom and justice for all" will remain a fantasy reserved only for white Americans. Racial "reconciliation" will never occur until black Americans own the same proportion of property across the nation as whites. And racism will persist as a national security problem until white Americans start seeing it as one.

I will next compare colonial Latvia's class system with the American racial caste system. I will compare the white American to the Baltic German, an ethnicity which no longer exists because of its refusal to relinquish privilege to a subservient group. Finally, I will discuss why I believe the Republican Party of the United States presents the greatest threat to America's viability in the 21st century.

In July of 2014, I sat over a glass of kefir with my Aunt Laila in the twilight of her Riga apartment. The drapes fluttered in the open windows (for some reason, Latvians do not use window screens) while pedestrians and motorcyclists alike rejoiced outside in the city's 20 hours of daylight. With my foreigner's naivety, perched at the kitchen table, I was asking Aunt Laila about the ongoing 'demographic crisis' in the country:

Since the fall of communism, Latvia, a country of two million, was shedding an average of 11,000 inhabitants per year, or 127,000 people in a decade, for better-paying jobs in the European Union.[4] Unabated by foreign immigration into an already ethnically diluted Latvia, the country's workforce is shrinking too quickly to support the country's burgeoning retiree population. So, in 2014, I perceived Latvians as squandering their independence and giving up on Latvia instead of rebuilding the country after its long-denied sovereignty. Furthermore, fears of slumping demographics coupled with a revanchist Vladimir Putin in 2014 alarmed me that someday there maybe wouldn't be enough people in Latvia to repel another Russian invasion.

Aunt Laila seemed indifferent, as if the demographic changes were the least of the country's worries. She recited an adage for me: "Stefan, we have a saying – 'Marry a Russian, for she will love you more deeply than any woman, or marry a Jew, for she will bear you more children, or marry a Latvian, for she will tend your grave longer than anyone on earth.'"

Indeed, Latvians have historically tended and beautified their family gravesites with the fervor of Japanese Zen gardeners. After

---

4 . ("Iedzīvotāju starptautiskā ilgtermiņa migrācija," 2022)

all, since two world wars and a 40-year Soviet occupation, I have learned, the specter of national extinction is omnipresent; today, there are even fewer Latvians alive than there were in 1914.

Half a year after my visit with Aunt Laila, I was driving across the snow-bound Rockies with my father on a road trip when he shared another anecdote about Latvians as unexpected as Aunt Laila's. "Hell is filled with a row of boiling kettles", my father said, "one kettle for Jews, one for Russians, and another for Latvians."

Around each kettle stands a devil with a pitchfork. These devils force the groaning souls back into the kettles as they try to escape. Only the Latvian kettle has no devil guarding it- it doesn't need one. As soon as any Latvian is about to climb from the kettle and escape, all the other Latvians join together to drag him back down.

Recalling my father's bizarre anecdote about hell's boiling kettles, in 2020, I was reading Isabel Wilkerson's book Caste, in which she writes: "Even as others in the lowest caste try to escape the basement, those left behind can tug at the ones trying to rise. Marginalized people across the world, including African Americans, call this phenomenon 'crabs in a barrel' (Wilkerson, 2020, pg. 240).

Indeed, just as my father's anecdote had foreshadowed similarities between the Latvian and black American experiences, Wilkerson introduced me to the "crabs in a barrel" analogy. In 2020, this prompted me to resume comparing Latvians and black Americans as I had in my teenage years.

In 2020, I learned that just as in colonial Latvia, when the Baltic German elevated the Latvian foreman ("vagars") above other serfs, the "Uncle Toms" and "HNIC's" ("head negroes in charge") in America enforced orders on the plantation. One Baltic German of the 18th century, Garlieb Merkel, described this phenomenon when writing: "If the Latvian manages to advance to a position of authority, such as becoming foreman or overseer of other Latvians, then he is even more sadistic than a German baron" (Merķelis, 2016, pg. 43).

As I learned in 2020, the similarities between colonial Latvian and the United States go even deeper than "crabs in a barrel" however. After Tsar Peter annexed Latvian lands from Sweden into the Russian Empire in 1710, he secured the loyalty of local Baltic German nobility by granting them unlimited privileges over the peasantry. From this point until World War I, the Russian Baltic and the American South mirrored one another remarkably well. Both were truly "countries within a country," codifying their laws and customs independent of Petrograd or Washington D.C. but relying heavily on unpaid labor. Both justified their human exploitation by stereotyping the lowest class according to an arbitrary difference (language in the Baltic, skin color in the United States) and institutionalizing these beliefs into culture. These institutions upheld beliefs for centuries about the lowest class's acceptable behaviors, attributes, and intelligence.

The stereotypes disfavoring colonial Latvians and black Americans were in many ways identical. Just as the 18th century's Latvian was insufferably lazy, constantly drunk and thieving, the stereotypical American slave was brutish, lazy, and simple-minded. Common stereotypes of black Americans today even still hold them to be lazy, criminal, and drug abusers. And just as the Baltic Germans implicated Latvians in their own poverty by "not spinning enough wool during the free time of winter," in the United States, Ronald Reagan implicated "welfare queens" as the source of black American poverty. Corporal punishment and whippings upheld the agrarian order on both the Southern plantation and the Baltic estate. Violence was necessary, the owner insisted, because the brutish slave or thieving Latvian was too undeveloped to understand other forms of discipline. And while Americans trafficked their property at Mississippi River ports, Riga's newspaper Rigische Anzeigen advertised Latvian serfs for sale. In both places, these advertisements highlighted the property's skills and robust physical stature, a "pleasant" or "docile" disposition, and nearly always concluded with a low price.

Beside corporal punishment and stereotypes, in the 18th, 19th, and 20th centuries, Baltic Germans and white Americans alike relied on policing and religion to uphold their social dominance. In both colonial Latvia and in the United States, the police foremost "protected and served" private property at the expense of the hierarchy's disposables.

Religion in the Baltic was as entwined with Baltic German supremacy as it was white supremacy in America.[5] Each Sunday, Lutheran ministers in Latvia preached that salvation awaited only the most docile and subservient Latvians, as they excluded disobedient or rebellious Latvians from burial in the hallowed church cemeteries.[6] As Latvian and Estonian peasants defected to Russian Orthodoxy in the 1840's to protest the Baltic German's Lutheran Church, prominent black Americans such as Cassius Marcellus Clay Jr. and Malcolm Little (Muhammad Ali and Malcolm X) rejected Anglo-Christianity for the Nation of Islam. This, of course, followed generations of Klansmen burning crosses in the yards of outspoken black Americans.

---

5. European and white Americans used the Biblical "Curse of Ham" to justify sentencing black people (the descendants of the son of Biblical Noah, Ham) to slavery.

6. Signifying the peasant's eternal obliteration.

A postcard from Jim-Crow Florida, titled "alligator bait," reinforcing American social values (Wikimedia Commons, 2022).

While reaping the benefits of unpaid labor, in both the American South and Russian Baltic, the upper classes poured their profits into lavish constructions while bemoaning even the smallest contribution to social welfare. From Virginia to Louisiana, cotton and tobacco funded the American antebellum architecture, while Baltic Germans pilfered from famine granaries to build their "allegorical gardens" or cover gambling debts. Today, tourist organizations paint a veneer of culture over these constructions in both places, nonetheless, a key difference remains. In the Baltic, where German supremacy was dismantled during the 1920 Agrarian Reform, tour guides don't romanticize or pigeonhole serfdom, unlike how many American plantation tours still treat slavery in the United States.[7]

---

7. An acquaintance once described their tour of a Southern plantation in South Carolina. They described "how well-cared for" the tour made the slaves appear, how the plantation tour advertised that many slaves "wanted to stay" after emancipation, before finally concluding that the tour presented how at least "one good thing" could come from slavery.

For decades leading up to inevitable emancipation, white Americans and Baltic Germans alike danced around their "agrarian questions." Whether doing so at the Baltic landtag or at congressional committees, conservatives within the upper class always managed to undermine meaningful reform. For instance, despite Baltic German conservatives harkening to Adam Smith when promising that serfdom would "work itself out" eventually, only federal intervention finally repealed servitude there in the 1810s. And although Baltic serfdom beat American slavery to abolition by 50 years, the result of "emancipation" in both places was the same– the dominant minority retained the land, while the subservient majority kept only "their time and their own two hands."[8]

Unable to rely on the "humanity" or "morality" of the slaveholder, both the Russian and American empires finally repealed indentured servitude across their whole territories in the 1860s. Nonetheless, Baltic Germans never committed treason against their government or waged war to preserve serfdom as white Americans did. And despite two "emancipations," generations of Latvians still streamed to Siberia for decades until World War I afterward to escape the dead-end Baltic. In the United States meanwhile, millions of black Americans emigrated from the Jim Crow South for the same reasons as Latvians, but at scales dwarfing Latvian emigration. This passive form of protest yielded tremendous labor shortages in both the Baltic and American South while throwing the very viability of the Latvian nation into question.

In the 1870s, when the federal government forced the Baltic Germans to begin selling land from their estates to peasants, the Baltic

---

8. After the Civil War and Reconstruction, Southern whites retained their plantations as the Baltic Germans kept their estates, leasing land to black American sharecroppers or Latvians in exchange for corvee.

Germans recouped their diminished land monopoly by extending century-term mortgages to the peasants. Forecasted as being unable to settle these debts until the 1960s, Latvian homeowners often lost entire investments because of one missed payment or a 'failed' home inspection. With their hard currency profits meanwhile, the Baltic Germans purchased factories in the rapidly industrializing Russian Empire. There, they re-enthralled the urban labor force, creating the abysmal conditions that galvanized the first leaders of the 1905 Revolution, the communist coup of 1917, and Latvia's 1920 Agrarian Reform.

By 1905, despite 'repealing' serfdom already twice, Baltic German supremacy persisted across Latvia as it had a century before. Although the Baltic Germans composed only 1.6% of Latvia's rural population, they still owned 54.1% of the land (Švābe, 1958, pg. 558), much like white Southerners retaining their plantations after the Civil War. Today in America, despite the civil rights legislation and desegregation of the South, three quarters of white Americans own their homes, while sixty percent of black Americans rent. This, by the way, is not the legacy of Southern slavery or Jim Crow, but of deliberate, racist redlining and loan denial to black Americans in the North. Racial inequities are alive and well in America, with disparities in property ownership and generational wealth for black Americans acute as they were in Latvia before the 1920 Agrarian Reform.

Despite the similarities linking the Latvian and black American struggles, several key differences remain. Simply put, in Latvia, Baltic Germans looked no different from Latvians. In colonial Latvia, most Baltic Germans spoke Latvian natively, since Baltic German toddlers learned Latvian lullabies from their nannies and wet nurses. With enough difficulty, effort, and luck meanwhile, Latvians could also sometimes Germanize to advance in society. In America, of course, the color of a person's face immediately advertised their position within the hierarchy. Black Americans could never change their skin color, not even to the power of six generations of ancestry according to American miscegenation laws. Thus, the main difference between colonial Latvia and the United States is one of modifiable social class versus immutable caste.

The other key difference is that the Latvian "question" was resolved after World War I with the radical 1920 Latvian Agrarian Reform. In the aftermath of World War I, the fledgling Latvian state nationalized all property in the country and redistributed it to landless peasants in equally sized parcels, without compensating the Baltic Germans for their losses. The Latvian state also created national monopolies over the country's forest, farmland, linen, and liquor to prevent private monopolies from forming. This deed was essentially a communist revolution in a single event, rather than as an ongoing, static process of governance as within the Soviet Union.

The opportunity for agrarian reform in Latvia only emerged with the simultaneous collapse of two adjacent empires- the Russian and German. In the United States, no such disruption has yet occurred. As a result, levels of black American home ownership, education, and health today lag far behind white Americans, while incarceration rates far exceed them.

Until 2020, I believed that the causes for this discrepancy remained innately within black Americans. Now, however, I've realized that the blame for black adversity lies entirely within white America; racial discrepancies have been codified into our very infrastructure and geography. Northern redlining, the continued hyper-policing of black communities, and the selective administration of laws and justice work in tandem to uphold the remnants of a caste system in America.

It was January of 2021. In the first year after a global pandemic, unprecedented presidential election, and George Floyd's murder by the police in my hometown, I had just finished reading Wilkerson's new book, Caste. In her book, published only a few months after George Floyd's murder, she wrote: "In the winter of 2020, the one year in human history that would hold the promise of perfect insight, an invisible life-form awakened in the Eastern Hemisphere." Indeed, amidst the anti-vaccination hysteria and Covid-denialism I'd witnessed in 2020, amidst Donald Trump goading the Republicans into an attempted coup of the United States government, I saw white Americans in 2020 for who we really are.

Despite my lifetime of evading responsibility for racism through my Latvian heritage, in 2020, I learned that by refusing to be anti-racist, I had only upheld the status quo all along- white supremacy. Until then, under a sage cloak of 'non-racism,' I had weaponized the Latvian "seven centuries of slavery" myth to diminish, defuse, and deny any black American outrage. By studying Latvian history from the DALV series in 2020 however, I learned that the notion of seven centuries' slavery for Latvians is entirely mythical, and that our ethnogenesis happened only because of political union under the hated Baltic Germans, not in spite of it. By studying Latvian and black American history in tandem, I also realized that perennial unrest does not smolder without reason. Furthermore, I learned that the black unrest and looting on Lake Street in Minneapolis was as legitimate as the Latvians nationalizing and redistributing all private property in their country a century earlier during the 1920 Agrarian Reform.

In the early spring of 2020, as I read about the Great Plague of 1711 following Russia's annexation of the Eastern Baltic, the first wave of Covid-19 arrived in America. During the plague, Latvian folk tales personified the pestilence as a "friendly dog with a silver bell," resounding amidst news reports that domestic animals could contract and spread Covid-19 back to humans. From my readings meanwhile, I learned that without the 1711 Plague, one-fifth of modern Latvia would still speak Livonian or Estonian today, two languages unintelligible and unrelated to the Indo-European ones like Latvian. Thus, my notion of a static and glorious Latvian nation occupying the eastern Baltic shore for 5,000 years was toppled.

Amidst the social disruption caused by a single strand of highly contagious RNA in 2020, American anti-intellectualism only further announced itself. The daily vitriol of Covid deniers undermined the Republicans' already baseless claims until then about a climate change hoax, Democrat voter fraud, Obama plotting a "Muslim takeover", and the "socialism" behind universal, affordable healthcare common in all other Western countries. From the highest office in the nation meanwhile, a white-nationalist president peddled his own cures for Covid, but only after stoking anti-Asian hatred with the "China virus."

As the initial lockdowns tapered in May of 2020, George Floyd's murder and the blatant white supremacy following it reared up again in the "progressive North."[9] Despite Floyd's (and onlookers') pleas for mercy that spring evening, the Minneapolis Police strangled Floyd on video for ten minutes between their knees and the curb— all over an alleged counterfeit twenty. After watching that footage, I recalled with shame and disgust my own "white moderate's" reaction in 2014,

---

9. Philando Castile's murder by Minnesota police in 2016 should have done this for me already; these officers were acquitted of all charges. Meanwhile, the dark- skinned Minneapolis police officer, Mohamed Noor, was convicted for crossing a sacrosanct boundary and killing a white woman, Justine Damond, in 2017.

when I'd criticized the black rage I found unpalatable. I remembered my refusal to acknowledge the ongoing, state-sanctioned violence which Black Lives Matter was drawing awareness to- that black Americans are guilty until proven innocent.

After Officer Chauvin so blatantly suffocated George Floyd in 2020, the fury and frustration of South Minneapolis exploded. Just a few blocks from my Latvian Church, from which I'd been borrowing installments of the DALV series, protesters began marching down Lake Street. As the first looters broke into K-mart amidst a social contract's interruption, young white paramilitaries swept into town from Texas to join the mayhem (Self-Described Member of "Boogaloo Bois" Charged with Riot, 2020). Minneapolis neighborhoods formed self-defense patrols, and the city's leadership issued warnings of "sophisticated urban warfare" before instating a curfew.

On the night of May 28, 2020, the Third Police Precinct erupted in flames.

Following George Floyd's murder and the release of his murderers – the police— Latvian Americans on social media betrayed their whiteness by defending private property over American lives.[10] 'He never should have been carrying that counterfeit 20-dollar bill," they insisted. "I support their cause, just not their tactics!"

This Latvian American response vexed me. As I'd been studying Latvian history, I learned that our ancestors had repeatedly burned and looted Baltic German private property, and that sometimes only violent uprising forced a change when the abuser wouldn't listen. Didn't the Latvians decrying Lake Street's unrest realize their hypocrisy, or had they forgotten that Latvia's 1920 Agrarian

---

10. Black American lives

Reform confiscated and redistributed all Baltic German estates without compensation?

In January 2021, after bleating without evidence for a month that the 2020 election was rigged against him, Donald Trump finally goaded his supporters into attacking the U.S. capitol to overturn the election. That January 6th, I watched as Republican lawmakers and traitors Ted Cruz, Josh Hawley, and Marjorie Taylor Greene 'removed their white hoods' to publicly support this attempted coup. Like Hitler's first failed Beer Hall Putsch, this time, the Republicans failed to overturn the election. Despite my grandparents' own experiences with societal collapse in Latvia during World War II, I nervously watched as other Latvian Americans on Facebook parroted Fox News' debunked talking points about 'voter fraud in Pennsylvania.'

2020 revealed to me the truth about myself that cousins in Latvia had been telling me since 2014, but which I refused to hear; that I am not really Latvian. In the year of perfect vision, I perceived myself and Latvian Americans at large for who we really are— just members of the dominant, white American caste.

Although many Latvian Americans romanticize the 1930s "Golden Age" of President Ulmanis, I know very few Latvian Americans who would ever tolerate "socialism" like universal, affordable healthcare in the United States, much less a radical property redistribution like 1920's Latvian Agrarian Reform. And despite professing their love for the restored Latvian and funding scholarships for Latvian American youth camps[11], many Latvian Americans proudly voted for a compromised, pro-Russian candidate in 2016 even when he trashed NATO security commitments. Indeed, despite Donald

11. Including my teenage heritage trip to Latvia in 2008.

Trump trashing these transatlantic security commitments during his presidency, in 2020, many Latvian Americans even doubled down and voted for him again, anyway.

In June of 2021, a few months after the Republicans' attempted coup had simmered, I attended a wedding in Saint Paul, Minnesota where I struck up a conversation with the event manager, a bouncer. This short yet intense, white, 30-year-old man scrolled through his Android phone to show me photos from his time fighting as a mercenary in Syria. After bashing Joe Biden to me and wrongly assuming I'd be sympathetic to this, he insisted that a second American Civil War was brewing.

I rolled my eyes. "There isn't going to be another civil war," I said. With a smugness gained from studying ten 1000-page volumes of Latvian history, I explained that war is a product of youth, not ideology, culture, or religion. Countries experiencing a "youth bulge," or when about 20% of the population is between 15 and 24, are highly volatile and susceptible to warfare. I linked a youth bulge in the Middle East, where the median age is around 22, to the 2011 Arab Spring and ISIS. I linked Latin America's youth bulge to Mexico's drug cartels, and Rwanda's 1994 genocide to a youth bulge there. Young people everywhere seek to overthrow old traditions of the previous generation; why else would Mao's "Cultural Revolution" have succeeded in China when it did? Why, after two world wars, has Western Europe experienced 80 unprecedented years of peace, if not for moving past its own youth bulge?

"America is simply too old to have another civil war," I concluded. "America is safe."

Despite my confidence in America's security at this present moment, one future question looms. In the coming decades, with a global population approaching 10 billion, and CO_2 emissions thawing Arctic methane, humanity faces its most dire challenge yet. A reorganization of generational wealth is meaningless when all the world's ocean-front condos are flooded by rising seas. Climate-change and crop failures in the 21st and 22nd centuries will dislodge waves of humanity that no border wall can withstand. And if a single, bat-borne strand of RNA disrupted the world like in 2020, what havoc can yearly droughts, famine, and sea level rise wreak?

Because of this climate change denialism, because it adheres to alternate 'realities,' and because it tried to overthrow the United States government in 2021, the Republican Party is now America's number one national security threat. Between conservative policies such as forced birth, denial of basic affordable healthcare, and wealth inequity not seen since the Gilded Age, Republicans and white nationalists will destroy this country the way the Baltic Germans destroyed themselves in Latvia during the 20th century. While I should have seen this from the Putin-Trump axis earlier, I didn't do more, partly because I didn't want to believe it. Nonetheless, continued Latvian American support for the Republican Party makes us even more complicit in this downfall.

Just as two centuries of Latvian peasant unrest did not quell until the 1920 Agrarian Reform dismantled Baltic German supremacy once and for all, reincarnations of black rage will not cease provoking "unpalatable" discussions until generational wealth is equalized in the United States. When property ownership between black and white Americans becomes proportional, then the remaining stereotypes and racial gaps will melt alongside it, as they did for Latvians.

As for the fate of the Baltic Germans; in 1796, a Baltic German named Garlieb Merkel forewarned of a terrible conflagration should the Latvian peasant finally break free of his chains. Nobody heeded Merkel, in fact they suppressed his message with a vehemence out-shadowing Fox News' diatribes against 'cancel culture.' For two centuries then, the Baltic Germans ignored or subverted reform. They chose personal wealth and privilege over their immortality. After the Bolshevik Revolution in 1917, the 1920 Latvian Agrarian Reform, and the expulsion of all Germans living east of the Oder in 1945, Eastern Europe today bears little resemblance to what it did in either 1796, 1914, or 1940.

In white America, meanwhile, a continued anxiety pervades us regarding minority hood "in our own country."[12] The 2020 Census corroborates this, showing that the number of Americans identifying solely as non-Hispanic "white" did not keep pace with the others, and even decreased. How will white America react to this ongoing demographic trend in the future? Will they follow the Baltic German example and seize power like Von der Goltz tried to do for the United Baltic Duchy against Latvia in 1919? Will they continue to overturn voting access for black Americans as they've done for a very long time, but have only ramped since 2020's Republican loss in Georgia? Will they even tolerate the popular vote in the future, or pursue an

---

12. This is a vile concern, as it considers black or any other type of American to not be truly "American", almost as if saying that All Lives didn't matter after all

even more gerrymandered Electoral College that already favors a white, conservative elite?[13]

If white Americans (including Latvian Americans) wish to avoid the Baltic German's fate, then we ought to start listening to black and native experiences about racism without defensiveness or "what about"-ism.[14] White supremacy is currently integral to this country's infrastructure, but it can also be dismantled, just as Baltic German supremacy was in Latvia after 1920.

When this country's stated ideals that "all men are created equal" finally match its four centuries of behavior, then this country will have fulfilled its destiny. After studying black history in 2020, I must say that America should be thankful black people only want equality, not revenge.

---

13. The 570 000 (mostly white) inhabitants of Wyoming hold two senate votes and one House representative, while the 750 000 (mostly black) inhabitants of Washington D.C. have no representation whatsoever. At the House of Representative and state government level, gerrymandered districts give Republicans artificial total control of the South and Midwest as well.

14. When I hear someone try to defend Russia after their 2022 invasion of Ukraine, or for any of their other tremendous crimes, I become infuriated to the point of trembling. This is probably a taste of what living under daily racism feels like for people of color in the United States.

Notes

The Latvian national myth, Lāčplēsis

In the late 19th century, a Latvian soldier in the Russian Imperial Army named Andrejs Pumpurs penned the Latvian national epic, *Lāčplēsis ("The Bear-Slayer")*. Drawing from Latvian folk tales inherited through the mythology of the extinct Livonian people, Pumpurs set his legend in the Daugava Canyon upstream from his native town at Lielvārde. Depicting Lāčplēsis as a hero with bear's ears that grant him superhuman strength, Lāčplēsis is the archetypal Latvian hero. During the national epic, Lāčplēsis fights to unite pagan Latvia and defend it from the duplicitous Christian missionaries of the 1200's- the forebearers of the hated Baltic Germans.

The legend begins as such: overlooking the River of Destiny, the Daugava in pre-Christian Latvia, a Latvian tribal chieftain paces along his wooden palisade at Lielvārde. As his son is coming of age, the two are discussing their kingdom's political concerns, the rising frequency of German traders and missionaries in the Baltic. Although these Germans claim to come for peaceful trade, the chieftain suspects otherwise.

As the father and son walk along, a bear suddenly lunges from the forest and knocks the chieftain to the ground. Rushing to defend his father, the son grips the bear by the jaws and tears them apart. Astonishing his father with this superhuman strength, the son is henceforth called "Lāčplēsis" – the bear-slayer. The chieftain then reveals his son's identity to him: as an infant, Lāčplēsis was found in the forest nursing from a bear. Because of these unique circumstances and because of his superhuman strength, the chieftain urges Lāčplēsis to depart home and become the great warrior he is certainly destined to be.

Travelling upstream toward the Daugava Canyon (now flooded behind the Pļaviņas Hydroelectric Dam) on the first day of his journey, Lāčplēsis rests at the hillfort of Aizkraukle. While the local chieftain here welcomes Lāčplēsis with traditional hospitality, his daughter, Princess Spīdala, seduces the hero. In addition to her "animalistic" beauty, Spīdala drapes herself in gems and jewelry unlike anything forged in pre-Christian Latvia. Being the archetypal hero he is, Lāčplēsis is determined to uncover the source of Spīdala's treasure.

Late one night, Lāčplēsis watches Spīdala from his castle window as she flies away on a magic log. She returns the next morning, before sunrise, bearing yet more gold. The following night, Lāčplēsis decides to hide inside the magic log and follow Spīdala. The enchanted log carries them up the Daugava Canyon before settling beside the mouth to a cavern; inside this cave, a witch's coven is feasting on snakes and boiled babies' hands as it prepares for a witch's sabbath.

After fornicating with demons they summoned for their ritual, the witches give an audience to Satan himself. The Devil announces his plan to use the cross-bearing Germans to enslave the Latvians. After the announcement is made and the sabbath is concluded, the eldest witch of the coven whispers to Spīdala that Lāčplēsis is hiding inside the log.

On her flight back to Aizkraukle, Spīdala jettisons Lāčplēsis into the Daugava, hoping to drown him. Staburadze, the goddess of the famous cliff Staburags, rescues Lāčplēsis. After restoring the hero to health in her crystal palace underneath the Daugava, Staburadze bestows the hero with a magic mirror he can use to fight his enemies. The next day, much to the Aizkraukle chieftain's joy (and Spīdala's fury) Lāčplēsis returns to Aizkraukle hale and hearty. From here, he bids farewell and continues onward to fulfill his destiny.

Lāčplēsis travels onward to Burtnieks, a military school in northern Latvia, where he befriends a soldier named Koknesis. Using his military training, Lāčplēsis defeats an evil Estonian giant and earns the princess Laimdota's hand in marriage for his heroism. Just as Lāčplēsis and Laimdota are due to wed, Spīdala kidnaps Laimdota, deporting her to a convent in Germany while framing Koknesis as the unrequited lover. Heartbroken and disillusioned, Lāčplēsis leaves Latvia to sail the northern seas.

As Lāčplēsis ventures north, Spīdala conjures a storm to blow him off course, so that Lāčplēsis' ship is cast beyond normal space and time. Beneath the aurora borealis, a spear-and-shield-toting Northern goddess instructs Lāčplēsis on the only way home, a circuitous path through lands full of monsters. After this journey, Lāčplēsis' ship finally lands on an island, which he discovers to be the home of Spīdala's coven. Laimdota and Koknesis are here too, although they have been turned to stone after escaping from Germany and being similarly blown off course.

Lāčplēsis chops down a golden apple tree at the center of the island, which destroys the eldest witch of Spīdala's coven. Spīdala emerges from the tree trunk and begs for mercy, repenting for her own sins. She releases the sailors who landed on the island but were turned to stone, among them Laimdota and Koknesis. Reunited with his love, Lāčplēsis proposes marriage again to Laimdota, while Koknesis asks for the reformed Spīdala's hand as well.

As the four friends return to pagan Latvia for their weddings, they discover their country preparing for war with the Crusaders. After the Latvians elect Lāčplēsis and Koknesis as their military commanders, the Latvian tribes finally unite under one banner to expel the Germans. Independence seems eternally ensured, and so Lāčplēsis marries Laimdota in a wedding ceremony according to pagan customs on the summer solstice.

Unfortunately, just like the Latvians in hell's boiling kettle, only another Latvian can betray Lāčplēsis. A witch doctor named Kangars reveals to the Germans that Lāčplēsis' strength resides in his bear-like ears. With this knowledge, the Germans send a knight wearing black armor to confront Lāčplēsis. The Black Knight challenges Lāčplēsis to a wrestling match, but when Lāčplēsis accepts it, the Black Knight swings at Lāčplēsis' bear-ears and cleaves them off with his sword.

Enraged, Lāčplēsis hurls the Black Knight over a cliff into the Daugava. Without his superhuman strength, however, he cannot maintain his footing and tumbles alongside the Black Knight. As Lāčplēsis plummets, Laimdota perishes, and Latvia's protectors are vanquished. Unimpeded, the Christian knights may now subjugate Latvia and enslave its people for the following centuries, as per the lines: "The Latvians, his beloved nation, toiled and slaved for centuries"[15] (Pumpurs, 1989, pg. 134).

The national myth concludes that all hope is not lost for the Latvians, however. From time to time, bargemen on the Daugava still report encountering the specters of Lāčplēsis and the Black Knight battling as they did 600 years before Andrejs Pumpurs wrote Lāčplēsis. As the same scene unfolds night after night in the moonlight, these specters collapse into the river together, neither able to defeat the other before disappearing together under the frothing water.

---

15. "Tauta, viņu mīļā tauta, Simtiem gadu vergoja."

The cliff, "Staburags," now underwater, photographed by the author on a beer can made by the Latvian brewery "Lāčplēsis," in 2018.

Although the legend of Lāčplēsis is clearly mythical, it gave 19th century Latvians a national past when none existed before. According to Lāčplēsis, Latvians were no longer a social class, but a nation, and one with a glorious past too. Ever since the Northern Crusades, Lāčplēsis insisted, the Baltic German had enslaved Latvians as serfs and stolen their land. Lāčplēsis thus legitimized the Latvian struggle against the Baltic Germans, while acknowledging the injustice of their ethnicity-based exclusion from property ownership. As a result, Latvians incorporated Lāčplēsis into their national identity.

In the modern republic of Latvia, you cannot visit a city or town without passing a "Lāčplēsis Street" or seeing a granite memorial depicting the mythical hero. The "Order of Lāčplēsis" was Latvia's highest military honor, awarded exclusively to heroes of the 1919 Latvian War of Independence. On November 11 every year since that time, crowds of Latvians have paraded with torches to commemorate "Lāčplēsis Day."

Through these monuments, honors, and holidays, the myth of Lāčplēsis is sometimes treated as historical fact in Latvia. I even derived the notion of seven centuries of Latvian enslavement from reading Lāčplēsis and listening to Gaismas Pils. The truth remains, however, that Lāčplēsis is an entirely mythical character, and that Latvia was never united politically (or linguistically) until the German Crusaders. Thus, I weaponized my heritage based upon a myth, using it only to diminish black American reports of racism in the United States.

The following map illustrates the tribes of 'Latvia' in the 13th century – the time of Lāčplēsis. Although I bristled in 1999 hearing Russian spoken in the steeple of St. Peter's church, the territory of modern Latvia was multi-ethnic long before it ever became 'Latvian.'

In the east, the blue Letgalians (the Latvians in Andrejs Pumpurs' mind) blocked marauding Slavs from encroaching into Baltic lands. Across the Daugava and south from Spīdala's castle near Staburags, the orange "highlanders" of Selonia blended with the highlanders (Aukštaiti) of Lithuania, suggesting they were one ethnos. "Selonia," the name Germans recorded in chronicles when they contacted the Livonians first of all the Baltic peoples, simply means 'highland' in the Livonian language. Even the Latvian-language term for this region, Augšzeme, means highland as well.

To the west, the neighboring "lowlanders" (the yellow Zemgaļi) merged with the similarly named region of Žemaitija in Lithuania.

Along the ice-free western coast, per medieval written records, the red Couronians spoke a language that was different from either Lithuanian or Latvian today but closer to the extinct Old Prussian language. Finally, the green group, the Finno-Ugric-speaking Livonians, are linguistic relatives of today's Estonians and Finns.

While Lāčplēsis claims to have united the Latvians against German aggression, much of Latvia's national myth is actually set in Livonian speaking lands and borrows its narrative from the legendary Finnic hero "Imauts." In 1198, near the mouth of the Daugava River, a Livonian-speaking leader named Imauts allegedly lanced the bishop Berthold of Hanover with his spear, routing the first crusaders (Ģērmanis, 1990, pg. 54-55). Deterred for a while, the crusaders eventually returned to defeat Imauts through trickery during a duel. The leaderless Livonians then scattered or surrendered, much as the apocryphal Latvians did after the Black Knight defeated Lāčplēsis.

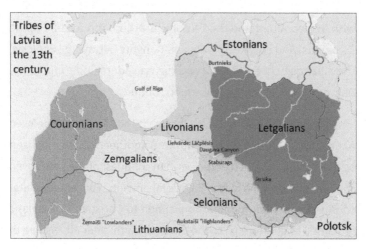

Image made by the author borrowing data from Turlajs (2005).

While the Livonians were the first tribe in the eastern Baltic to adopt Roman Catholicism, Lāčplēsis also misleads historiography when it insists that all the other Baltic peoples remained pagans in the 13th century. Upstream from Riga on the Daugava River, the Letgalian chiefdoms of Koknese and Jersika had embraced Orthodox Christianity from the Slavs in Polotsk before the Crusaders' arrived (Ģērmanis, 1990, pg. 66). In 1209, Bishop Albert of Riga even marched to the mightiest of these fortresses at Jersika, torched the hillfort, and reoriented Latvia toward Western Europe by incinerating Orthodoxy there in an instant[16] (Ģērmanis, 1990, pg. 65-69).

Where Lāčplēsis aligns better with historical chronicles is in its presentation of the endemic warfare between proto-Latvian tribes and Estonians. In the national epic, Lāčplēsis must defeat Kalapuisis, the evil Estonian giant, to earn Laimdota's hand in marriage. In reality, prior to political union of the German crusaders, the Estonians and Letgalian tribes waged ongoing, intertribal blood-feuds. Their mutual hatred ran so deeply that in 1208, the Letgalian tribe of Tālava allied with Bishop Albert and the Teutonic Brotherhood to subdue the Estonians. And so, like Spīdala and Kangars betraying Lāčplēsis, the alliance between Tālava and the crusaders undermined the Baltic's entire resistance to German conquest.

Although Lāčplēsis ends with the lines "The Latvians, his beloved nation, toiled and slaved for centuries," another myth popularized by the national epic is that the German conquest of the Baltic even changed everyday life for the Baltic's inhabitants. For centuries after conquest and their nominal conversion to Christianity, Latvians remained largely foreign to the Christian faith; after all, instead of

---

16. The "Gospel of Jersika", a translation of the Gospel into Old Church Slavonic, was written in Letgalian tribal lands around 1270 and is archived today in Russia.

spreading the Gospel to pagans, the young crusaders from Saxony were much more interested in gaining tribute, wives, and defending their fortresses. So, in exchange for military allegiance and nominal conversion to Christianity, most German leadership extended the kingdoms back to the Baltic tribal leaders as fiefs, from which they continued to govern uninterrupted as before the crusades.

Even after the arson and fall of Jersika in 1209, King Visvaldis was invited to Riga and offered his old dominion back in exchange for an oath of loyalty and nominal conversion to Catholicism. When the Couronians surrendered in the 1260's, they kept their privileges to maintain their sacred, pagan groves if they provided mounted soldiers to the German crusaders during wartime. These "Kings of Courland" (Kuršu Koniņi) maintained their private property into modern times, playing the ethnic Latvian's closest analog to "nobility".[17]

For the proto-Latvian peasants meanwhile, the arrival of feudalism certainly didn't mean automatic enslavement either. During the three centuries of the Livonian Confederacy's existence, chronic warfare with Lithuania and Muscovy provided a steady supply of prisoners to use when building Livonia's stone castles. In contrast to Lāčplēsis' melodramatic enslavement myth, two different forms of serfdom actually existed in Latvia over the centuries— the forms before and after 1710, when Tsar Peter annexed the Baltic to Russia.

In the lighter, earlier form of serfdom characteristic of medieval times, each head of household paid tribute to the landlord of the estate, normally $1/10^{th}$ of his farm produce, while keeping the right

17. Under feudalism, most vassals received land from the bishop as a fief for the duration of the vassal's lifetime; when the vassal died, the fief returned to the bishop's ownership rather than passing on through inheritance. In Latvia, only the Kings of Courland inherited their fathers' properties without intercession of the bishop.

to remain in his generational home as private property (Dunsdorfs, 1964, pg. 438). Today, we pay taxes in much the same way.

In the heavier form of Baltic serfdom during colonial times, every head of household had obligations- often only achievable through starvation and sleep deprivation- while lacking the right to remain in his generational home should the noble wish to evict him. Historian Edgars Dunsdorfs equated this second form of serfdom with 'slavery' and characterized it only for those Latvians living in the 18th century Russian Empire (Dunsdorfs, 1962, pg. 264). Thus, the medieval period of Latvian history can hardly be considered the beginning of seven centuries' continuous enslavement.

Finally, while Lāčplēsis purports that the arrival of the Germans commenced a seven-century "night" for the Latvians, in truth, without political incorporation into the Livonian Confederation, the tribes of the Eastern Baltic probably wouldn't identify as Latvian today. During an earlier age, for commerce and inter-ethnic communication, the Orthodox Letgalians and Estonians would have likely adopted Old Church Slavonic in the way Latin became the lingua franca for the West. This same phenomenon had already happened to the Baltic tribes living on the Dnieper River in Belarus and the Finns along the Volga near Moscow. Therefore, without a German interruption, the eastern Baltic would probably speak something more akin to Russian or Belarusian due to shared religion. But because of the Northern Crusades, the Livonian Order effectively halted Slavic linguistic expansion to the West (Šterns, 1997, pg. 416). Latvians, therefore, exist because of a political union under the earliest Baltic Germans, that unforgivable "enemy" in Lāčplēsis.

Die Letten

In the 1800s, the Latvians were among the most literate ethnicities in the Russian Empire, alongside Estonians. Literacy often exceeded 90% of the population across the Latvian and Estonian countryside, while it hovered around 50% in Lithuania, 30% in Belarus, and below 20% in ethnically Russian provinces (Turlajs, 2005, pg. 35). By the turn of the 20th century, Latvians were also becoming global travelers; waves of them emigrated annually to virgin fields as far as the Ukrainian steppes or Siberia to escape the ethno-class hierarchy in the Baltic. Latvian laborers laying tracks for the Trans-Siberian railroad later rode these trains to the end of the line to establish Latvian colonies on the Russian Pacific coast.

Unlike these "cosmopolitan" Latvians of the 1800s, the Latvians in the 1700s were among the dimmest of nations, living no better than livestock bound to the estates that they cultivated. There was no honor in being Latvian at this time. All throughout the 1700s, the term Latvian (ein Lette) was interchangeable with the term for "peasant" (ein Bauer), and both could be used equally to insult someone as much as designate their ethnicity. In the 1700s, the Latvians were no more than a social class, certainly not a nation with a past or a future; it is illustrative that, until the 1870s, the Latvian language lacked words to even designate concepts such as 'past' or 'future,' until Latvian linguists invented them during the 19th century's First National Awakening (Švābe, 1958, pg. 405).

At the end of the 1700s, a young Baltic German named Garlieb Merkel witnessed first-hand how indentured servitude had dehumanized the peasantry in his native Livonia province northeast of Riga. The son of a local Lutheran minister, Merkel found Livonian serfdom incompatible with the Enlightenment ideals and the writings of his education. This inspired him to pen Die Letten ("The Latvians") in 1796, in which he depicted the institution of Latvian chattel serfdom as it existed at that time.

Written originally in German and suppressed from publication in Latvian until 1905, Merkel's treatise demanded the liberation of the Latvian peasantry from serfdom. According to the Enlightenment's Universal Rights of Man, Merkel insisted, Latvians could not remain 'objects' owned by the nobility, bred and utilized for fieldwork as livestock. Indeed, until the end of the 18th century, Latvians were trafficked and sold at markets, advertised in newspapers and classifieds ads, and "mated" for desirable qualities and plentiful offspring.

Due to the nobility's stranglehold over Baltic society however, no business in Riga would consider publishing Merkel's radical manuscript. Thus, in 1797, Merkel turned to publishers in liberal Leipzig, Germany. When the first editions from Leipzig arrived in Riga, so entrenched was serfdom to the Baltic economy that the nobility quietly purchased all copies from bookstores and destroyed them to suppress Merkel's message. From the few surviving copies that managed to circulate, Die Letten provoked a reaction among conservative Baltic Germans more visceral than modern American reacting to 'abolish the police.' In its time, Die Letten provoked snarling hostility more analogous to that after Uncle Tom's Cabin circulated in the United States in the 1850s.

Die Letten began with a summary of Latvian history, or at least the "history" that inspired Lāčplēsis, which I showed in the last section to be apocryphal. Merkel wrote that in the 1100s, merchants from Bremen disembarked on the Baltic's eastern shores, traded with Latvian pagan tribes, and returned to Christendom. Unable to resist an easy conquest however, they returned brandishing swords and the Holy Cross; according to Merkel, ministers preaching "Christianity" achieved more than the sword in that era, as the Latvian forefathers surrendered their worldly possessions blindly to promises of euphoria in the afterlife.

Merkel wrote: "Six centuries since the Latvians plunged into slavery- this significant period of time, when all other nations have made admirable strides to fulfillment, the Latvians and Estonians remain mired in place... Latvians today wander along, knowing no happiness beyond whole-heartedly gnawing their chaff-bread, knowing no courage greater than daring to meet their master's gaze, knowing no cleverness other than to avoid being caught in a theft. The Latvian considers himself virtuous for limiting his binge-drinking to once per week, considers it his greatest honor to avoid another whipping. In a word, anyone could be a Latvian if their humanity had been gnawed by six centuries of enslavement" (Merķelis, 2016, pg. 26, 48).

After describing the period of bondage that lasted six centuries (from 1200-1796), Die Letten illustrated the Latvian's relationship with the Baltic German landlord, his master and keeper. "The most vivid attributes I can ascribe to the Latvians is their slave-like fear and mistrust of all that is German. Passing his master at thirty feet, even trudging by his master's home, the Latvian removes his hat and shrinks like a wood louse. You couldn't call it a bow. With a drooping head and retracted neck, he lobs along to kiss his master's coat and shoes" (Merķelis, 2016, pg. 30).

Similarly, Merkel described how the word 'German' is used in conversation by Latvians to describe anything arrogant, miserly, or wicked – in a word, anything hated. "Oh, you stupid German!"

a Latvian woman curses her milking cow after being kicked to the ground and spilling the pail. "Quiet now – or the German will come!" a Latvian nanny might hush a toddler the way baby-sitters elsewhere warn of bogeymen.

"When spoken to by his master," Merkel wrote, "the Latvian ponders every word of the statement for trickery, answering as evasively as possible. A thousand experiences have taught him how easily a misspoken word can expose a vulnerability, which the German baron will readily exploit. Overall, the Latvian will accept only that which can be given and not revoked, that is, something to be eaten or drank" (Merķelis, 2016, pg. 30).

Touching upon the endemic violence of Latvians, Merkel cited an incident whereby twice in a single year, a pair of starving boys beat their parents to a pulp before turning on one another. At another estate, a Latvian farmer locked his family in their home without food, refusing even to give up the house key, so that he might drink uninterrupted in the nearby tavern. Sent by the farmer's wife, the farmer's brother then struck the farmer down on the road home, bludgeoned his head with a club, and castrated him with a bread knife.

Merkel described the Latvian's primary 'occupation' after agriculture – alcoholism. "Among grown men and women, you will rarely find one who does not get drunk each Sunday, particularly if Eucharist was given that day. If a Latvian cannot afford to drink, the man will sell the groceries from his home, the woman – her clothes" (Merķelis, 2016, pg. 32). Gently cooing, a Latvian mother might sip vodka from a glass while nursing her infant, and 14-year-old Latvians shoot spirits without squinting at all. Alcohol was easily accessible, mass-produced by the estates, and numbed the Latvian peasants enough for momentary escape.

While the landowning Baltic Germans of the 1700's lavished in the profits of uncompensated labor and vodka sales, constructing mansions and allegorical gardens, the Latvians funding this institution lived no better than livestock. "The peasants inhabit farmsteads scattered in in the woods, a single door requiring one bend low to enter. Without chimneys or windows, whole families slept and ate together on rags amongst their pigs, chickens, and dogs. Hearth smoke permeated all corners of the windowless one-room shack, searing the eyes of newborn babies" (Merķelis, 2016, pg. 27).

Tradition and laws guaranteed the noble could evict households from generational homes on whatever pretext, sending them to clear new fields in the forest. Whether out of greed or vengeance against an outspoken peasant, the baron could raze an evicted tenant's home mid-winter and summon him back in spring to cultivate grain on former flower beds.

Die Letten commented on the 'backwardness' of the Latvian peasant in the 18th century, his anti-intellectualism, resistance to modernity, and insularism. Colonial Latvians would be considered virulent anti-vaxxers today, foregoing inoculations to simply cut off smallpox scabs and serve them to their children on bread ("Better the child die now than eating more than his share and die later" (Merķelis, 2016, pg. 37)). If a Latvian encountered a foreigner on a road, he quarreled with, gawked at, mocked, or deliberately misled the stranger. Despite five centuries in Western Christendom, Latvians of the 18th century still practiced fortune-telling and magic, honored house spirits, and sacrificed small animals at hills, groves, caves, or springs. Modernity in agriculture (the potato, clover) meant nothing to the Latvian except another method for barons to squeeze out free labor, to "fertilize the peasants like manure on the fields" (mēslot savus zemniekus).

In the 18th century, a typical growing season for the Latvian was as follows: corvee (rent-labor) four days per week and personal fieldwork on the remaining two. Sundays were reserved for rest, but more frequently spent salvaging household crops due to the sheer exhaustion from the previous four days working on the estate. During the summer, the Latvian peasant tilled, sowed, mowed, weeded, and harvested the estate's grain as part of his obligations before his own crops. The Latvian labored on the estate with his own horses and equipment, sustained himself with his own provisions ("savā maizē"). Rain days required the peasant make up for missed estate fieldwork on the weekends. As a result, hay for the peasant's personal livestock often rotted unattended in the fields, weeds overran the peasant's cereals, and over-ripened grain for personal consumption burst uselessly into the soil at harvest. Under normal agrarian conditions, famines should have been rare occurrences in the Baltic, but in colonial Livonia and Estonia, famine arrived each spring as reliably as the first robin.

In addition to the four days a week of corvee codified as a noble right, barons classified essential activities such as hauling and spreading manure, running postal errands, repairing roads, and splitting rock as "extraordinary jobs" not counting towards normal corvee. Normally, they coerced Latvian peasants into this by threatening them with eviction. Other times, Baltic German barons rewarded their peasants for a completed job, called a "talka" in Latvian, with leftover beer and home-made moonshine for boorish drinking-binges.

After the fall's cornucopia, the Latvian peasants behaved like overnight millionaires, throwing weddings and staggering drunkenly from farmstead to farmstead. After all, what good is frugality to someone excluded from building wealth by the existing order? What does thriftiness matter to someone who can be evicted at a moment's notice, who's own children will live no better than the parent? More concerned about lost productivity and wasted inventory, the Baltic German barons drafted legislation to regulate how much a Latvian could spend on a wedding, including how many invitations he could extend and how to best concentrate weddings into one week of the year to limit productivity loss from hangovers.

Thus, the stereotype of the 'lazy' Latvian emerged at this time for much similar reasons as it did for the black American slave or sharecropper: exhaustion. "It is no surprise," historian A. Johansons wrote, "the peasant was lazy and aloof to his work; he barely moved when noticing the pigs digging through his recently sowed vegetable beds, or the cattle trampling the grain" (Johansons, 1975, pg. 12).

In the 1700s, another stereotype of Latvians arose: their innate drive to thievery and criminality. 'Work theft' was unavoidably common when all a peasant's personal effects were considered 'loaned' from the baron, and his personal autonomy was non-existent. Tolerance of theft became institutionalized as a means of dividing the peasantry- the poorest peasants were hired as quartermasters with the expectation that they would steal inventory and become the most ardently loyal servants. These peasants could then be promoted into foremen ("vagari"), who gladly dispensed whippings and absolve their Baltic German masters of playing the devil around the Latvian kettle.

After reveling through the wedding season, during the dark half of the year, "the peasant finally hibernates in every meaning of the word" (Johansons, 1975, pg. 78). Even if mowing and weeding ended at the harvest, it didn't absolve the peasant of wintertime corvee. Over winter, the peasant was expected to cut timber for estate distilleries, run postal errands on frozen roads, spin wool at the wheel, and transport wagon loads of alcohol to market, all on one's "own bread" again. Latvian peasants frequently lost horses to exhaustion during these winter assignments and assumed high-interest loans to replace the mares.

Hunger returned in spring as the last of the stored grain was spent. Peasants cut their daily bread with chaff (pelavas) or scraped together whatever flour dust and mouse droppings they could to boil a porridge. Retching against "welfare," meanwhile, the Baltic German nobility circumvented federal efforts to ensure against famine by bribing granary supervisors for grain that they could distill into yet more vodka. Die Letten recalls an otherwise able-bodied, 18-year-old Latvian wallowing in the streets, staving off starvation by swallowing clods of mud off the main road because of empty granaries.

To avoid a complete famine altogether, German barons reluctantly extended grain to peasants from their private stores (stolen from the granaries) but only as high-interest loans. Thus, like a gravity well from which not even light could escape, the already penniless Latvian fell into inescapable debt-bondage after only a few seasons.

During the Great Northern War, Tsar Peter extended privileges and autonomy to Baltic German nobles of Livonia in exchange that they switch their loyalty from Sweden to Russia. After this war, the Baltic German nobles monopolized not only the farmland, but also held the sole rights to timber, pastures, fishing, hunting, distilling spirits, and operating flour mills. They managed to deprive Latvians not only of property ownership, but also of owning personal effects, grinding their own flour, and maintaining full autonomy of their bodies. Corporal punishment upheld this class-based hierarchy. During the 1700s, a Latvian saying arose: "viņš tad laikām tikai gājis pēc rīkstēm", meaning that, should a Latvian peasant complain about a landlord's directive or ruling, onlookers only pitied him for the flogging he was due to receive (Johansons, 1975, pg. 41).

Through whippings, the barons dispatched rebellious Latvians, sometimes arbitrarily to gaslight the peasantry like electric-shocked rats. The nobles codified and legalized corporal punishment as their "rights to home discipline" (mājas pārmācības tiesības), justifying them as a necessary component of law and order. "Desmit rīkstes" was a common punishment dispensed, whereby peasants received floggings with a set of ten switches, three hits per switch, or until they snapped. More frequently, the floggings lasted "until the peasant's flesh tumbled to the floor" and there was nothing left to thrash (Merķelis, 2016, pg. 86). Floggings could be repeated weekly to intimidate, terrorize, and subdue.

Conservative Baltic Germans compared corporal punishment to a father disciplining his children, emphasizing that it was a 'sparingly used' method for upholding law and order. Die Letten contradicts this, citing instances whereby one Latvian peasant girl was thrashed for her 'sloppy folding' of linens, and another maiden was flogged for refusing the sexual advances of her landlord. Latvian men received "ten switches" for defending their wives from rape or for insubordination. Many times, "home discipline" precluded outright sadism.

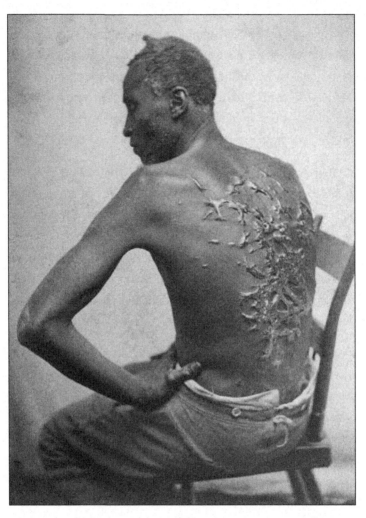

This photo of "Whipped Peter," a runaway slave in the United States, indicates what the "rights to home discipline" were capable of (Wikimedia Commons, 2022).

Die Letten described Latvian maiden who once poorly completed a household task. The baroness, unsatisfied with the maiden's work, wrapped linen bandages around the maiden's fingertips and set them aflame. Naturally, the maiden couldn't spin wool better with raw and blistered fingertips, but due to her continued clumsiness, the baroness administered thrashings with switches soaked in salt-water. For whatever perceived 'last-straw,' the baroness finally imprisoned the maiden in a cellar. Here, the baroness tied the maiden's wrists to the walls, her hands given food and water to hold. The ropes, of course, restrained the girl from bringing the food to her mouth to eat.

Merkel acknowledged that not all estates abused their peasants in this manner, a tip to conservative Baltic Germans who might otherwise scream "not all barons!" like modern defenders of American policing. Some Latvian peasants lived so well as to wear the latest petticoats from Riga, never once enduring eviction from their generational homes. On one estate, a Latvian wasn't flogged even after crossing the sacrosanct class boundary of punching his Baltic German master.

This highlights the divisive, erratic nature of Baltic serfdom, whereby the peasant's entire well-being was dependent on his master.[18] If an estate's fortunes rose, so did the peasant's. If a tyrannical foreman drove his serfs to the woods, then likewise, the remaining peasants assumed still more corvee and deprivation. Migration to better employers was outlawed except with noble permission, often through sale or as a gift. Runaway Latvians were compared to property with legs. And the Latvians and Estonians most able to mount resistance to their captivity, the prosperous and materially stable ones, needed only gaze at the rags of chronically starving neighbors before bowing their own heads back down.

"The peasant of Livonia," Merkel concluded, "will remain a thief and a swindler for as long as he remains maltreated and scrambles

---

18. In the United States, the black American must continuously "read into" the intentions of every white American, lest the police become involved

for a daily existence. It is the only avenue by which he can drag himself along, momentarily achieve a sense of stability and success" (Merķelis, 2016, pg. 44).

Written shortly after the French Revolution, Die Letten declared that the Enlightenment's Universal Rights of Man applied to every Latvian and Estonian, earning Merkel insults such as "French Jacobin" from conservative Baltic Germans.[19] These Enlightenment rights included the inalienable right to personal belongings, the right to freedom from human trafficking, the right to be free of excessive punishment, and the right to choose one's spouse rather than have arranged breeding. Merkel declared that every peasant also had the right to an impartial hearing in court; at the time of Die Letten, peasant tribunals ended as show-trials, usually with gaslighting and more "home discipline."[20] Merkel asserted that Latvians had a right to granaries untampered with by the nobility as insurance against famine. Furthermore, peasants had the right to freedom from medical experiments; Die Letten cites one baroness who treated broken bones with emetics like rhubarb. As a result of being force-fed rhubarb for a chest injury, the Latvian peasant's stomach convulsions disrupted his bandages and he bled to death in the barn.[21]

Merkel cited the swinging guillotines of France in his warning to Baltic Germans about the price of ignoring Rousseau's Social Contract. Long before 1917's communist revolution or the 1920 Agrarian Reform, Merkel discerned within the Latvians a "caged tiger waiting to someday wash its keeper in blood." He quoted a Latvian

19. Probably analogous to a Republican calling affordable healthcare "socialism" today.

20. Compare to black Americans facing all-white juries.

21. From the 1930s to the 1970, the United States government deliberately infected black Americans with syphilis as part of its Tuskegee Syphilis Study, showing just how expendable the Baltic Germans and the United States considered their subordinates.

peasant in saying: "Who? The true Master of this land? He sits above us in Heaven, and his Vicar sits on the throne in Petrograd. These others deserve only to be bludgeoned and left for dogs to devour in the streets" (Merķelis, 2016, pg. 119). Thus, Merkel argued, the persistence of serfdom, aside from its inhumanity, also presented an existential threat for Baltic Germans.

Establishing that the Livonian social order would one day change, Die Letten proposed a choice for his readers; either the Baltic German nobility willingly sacrifice some privileges now or suffer a conflagration consuming their entire corporation later. It was a prophecy of sorts, since after Russia's Communist Revolution, the 1920 Agrarian Reform in Latvia, and Hitler's failed war, the Baltic Germans no longer exist today. In 1920, the Latvian Republic nationalized all property and re-distributed farms amongst the citizens; no Baltic Germans were compensated for their losses. In 1939, Hitler ordered all ethnic Germans back to the Third Reich, and those who didn't were expelled from Eastern Europe by the Red Army anyway. By 1950, 12 million ethnic Germans had left Eastern Europe, not only from the Baltic States but also from half of modern Poland's territory. Latvia's current German population numbers 3,000, even less than the number of remaining Jewish people there since the Holocaust.

Merkel acknowledged that arrogance alone did not make nobles monsters; many Baltic Germans depended upon serfdom for their financial security and to avoid bankruptcy. Although some of Latvia's most ornate palaces and manors were built in the 18th century, these estates also traded hands like stocks in Rotterdam. Some were sub-leased to profit-seekers and speculators while the owners eloped, others auctioned at inflated prices or purchased solely on credit. This allure of a quick profit tempted adventurists into subprime mortgages; to avoid defaulting on their own obligations, they brutalized their peasantry more than any 'matriculated'[22] German noble.

Finally, Die Letten engaged the counterarguments most often lobbed against serfdom's abolition. The Latvians were too lazy, conservatives warned, too wasteful and childlike to properly enjoy freedom. Latvian peasants were 'too drunken' and 'thieving' for freedom, too quarrelsome and too prone to violence. Abolishing serfdom, conservatives argued, would be like "putting a shaving knife in the hands of an infant" (Johansons, 1975, pg. 30). It is worth noting that the Latvians, among the most literate nationalities of the Russian Empire a century later, were considered 'too simple and undeveloped' for freedom in the 1700s.

Die Letten dispatched these stereotypes one by one and placed the blame for the Latvian's decayed life squarely on the shoulders of Baltic Germans.[23] "Even the Romans acknowledged that someone who has lost his freedom has also lost half of his humanity" (Merķelis, 2016, pg. 140).

"Ignore my warnings," Die Letten concluded, "and only a catastrophe will decide the Latvian's fate. I lay this treatise before humanity's eyes as a testament to the terrible trial which, sooner or later, will judge you oppressors. And may the future convict you! Tremble, you tyrant brothers – it will convict you terribly, and soon!" (Merķelis, 2016, pg. 160)

As previously mentioned, Die Letten's publication into the Latvian language was suppressed for over a century. Politicians and censors

22. Registered in a list certifying noble origin.
23.In a similar way, white Americans and racist lending practices alone are responsible for the 'blighted' inner-city ghettos of the Northern United States.

officially cited this treatise as a being a risk for inciting unrest. Nonetheless, Die Letten still circulated amongst literate Latvian peasants during the 1800s through hand-written translations. Historian Gvido Straube suggested that Die Letten's content was known to organizers of the 1802 Latvian peasant uprisings at Kauguri, the revolts which finally pressed lawmakers into reforming Baltic serfdom. Die Letten's claims of six centuries enslavement also resounded with Latvian readers, who incorporated it into their poetry and literature (Lāčplēsis, Gaismas Pils) during the First National Awakening sixty years later.

Almost immediately following the first readings of Die Letten in Riga, conservative Baltic Germans launched over 250 press articles denouncing the treatise and attacking Merkel ad hominem. Their diatribes equated Merkel with the guillotine-pulling Jacobins, called him a fibber, and depicted him as an ungrateful schoolboy who was avenging himself for feeling cheated by life. The attacks against Merkel never fully ceased until after World War Two when nearly all Baltic Germans had finally repatriated or been expelled.

Western Europeans audiences, by contrast, applauded Die Letten. Translators at Germany's University of Jena raced to compose German, French, and Danish editions. Academics fraternized with the author, appealing to him for an audience at their corporations. French ambassadors invited Merkel to serve alongside them in Paris. Although his membership to the Freemasons largely shielded him from being blacklisted by Baltic society, Merkel nonetheless remained in Frankfurt and Berlin as a journalist for the rest of his life, only returning to Livonia in his retirement.

The legacy of Die Letten, much like the Black Lives Matter movement today, was one of stirring the ignorant public's awareness to ongoing abuse of power. However, just as the police who murdered George Floyd surely would never have been arrested or prosecuted without the 2020 Minneapolis riots, repealing serfdom would have remained shelved for decades unless Latvian peasants themselves burned, looted, and torched manors for half a century. Die Letten and Black Lives Matter created platforms to speak out against injustice, nonetheless, Latvian history shows that in class or caste systems, words without action do not produce change.

The 18th Century in Colonial Latvia

In 1703, as the Russian and Swedish Empires waged the Great Northern War for hegemony of the Baltic Sea, Tsar Peter captured the Swedish fortress of Nyenschantz on the Gulf of Finland. From the surrounding marshes, he conscripted Russian and Finnish peasants to erect a stone fortress here and solidify Russian control of the strategic Neva delta. Through this "window to Europe," Peter named Russia's new port in the style of a good European city, calling it Sankt-Pieter-Burch until the communists renamed it 'Leningrad' two centuries later. Though accessible to the ocean via the Gulf of Finland, St Petersburg still remained ice-bound for half the year, and Tsar Peter had to gaze further south for a warmer, ice-free port.

In 1710, with the capitulation of Riga, Tsar Peter finally shattered the Swedish Empire's hegemony of the Baltic Sea, although the war continued for another decade. With Sweden's loss of Riga, the Baltic was no longer a "Swedish Lake" but a barrier dividing Eastern Christendom from West. Despite promising Livonia and Estonia to Sweden's rival Poland at the war's outset, Tsar Peter reneged and annexed the provinces directly to the Russian empire. These new maritime provinces remained exposed to Swedish counterattacks, and so Peter secured them by purchasing the local nobility's loyalty in event of counter-invasion.

In exchange for their Russian allegiance, Tsar Peter granted the Baltic Germans historically unseen dominion over the Latvian and Estonian peasants. In 1712, the Russian "Plowshare Review" dismantled the nationalized estates of Sweden which protected peasants from abuse and converted them directly into private property of the Baltic German nobility. This Plowshare Review classified all peasants as property of the estate they inhabited, compelling them to perform daily corvee as rent to remain in their homes. Legally, the nobility could now arbitrate over peasant's marriages, bodies, lives, and deaths. In securing the Baltic provinces for the Russian Empire, Tsar Peter rendered generations of Latvians and Estonians to the level of breeding livestock.

As Riga capitulated in 1710, a plague swept into the eastern Baltic. Already convulsed by the war, the peasants believed this pestilence to be God's wrath and refused to perform their fieldwork. Public gallows did little to motivate those expecting Armageddon at any moment. As a result, crops remained untended, and famine claimed the remaining peasants who'd escaped the plague. Latvian historians estimate that the combined Great Northern War, plague, and famine claimed two-thirds of the Baltic's peasantry, while erasing the last speakers of the Livonian language from the eastern shore of the Gulf of Riga (Dunsdorfs, 1962, pg. 13) (Dunsdorfs, 1973, pg. 278, 282, 296).

Surrounded by marauding troops and mass pestilence, ethnic Latvians fled to forests and bogs along the coast. They settled along the Bay of Riga, recently emptied of its Finnic-speaking Livonians by the plague, and "Latvianized" these former fishing villages. Because of this, towns viewed today as quintessentially Latvian, such as Limbaži, Salacgrīva, and Sigulda, share little in common with their medieval, Livonian-speaking past.

After the war, local pastors and officials described the mood in Livonia as "apocalyptic" (Johansons, 1975, pg. 14). Shrubbery overtook farmsteads while roofs of empty cottages collapsed under winter rains. Feral animals scavenged for leftover grain amidst unburied skeletons. Without congregations surviving to reinforce Christianity, the remaining peasants returned to a Christian-pagan syncretism of their ancestors. Their rituals personified natural forces as the saints, and Latvians cast spells with words recalled from the Christian litanies.

Because of the plague's demographic convulsions, the Latvians' "seven centuries of slavery" truly began only in 1710 with Tsar Peter's conquest and the unlimited privileges granted to Baltic Germans. After mass mortality claimed local historians, few Latvians survived to inform the next generations about life before the plague.[24] Sometimes, elders brought their sons to the forest and pointed out long-gone farmsteads recalled from childhood. Other times, Latvian children's fables personified the plague as a "friendly dog with a bell on its collar." But beyond these cultural memories, local Latvian peasants could only behold Latvian history like the medieval castle ruins around them – with exotic wonder.

In the local conception of Latvian history, the very first Baltic Germans- the bishops, knights, and nobles of medieval Livonia- became equated with the tyrants of the 18th century. Never mind that generations of war and empire-building had separated the stained-glass bishops from the contemporary barons. Also, the Baltic Germans of the 18th century directly benefited from this centuries-of-enslavement myth when legitimizing their economic supremacy, and so actively promoted it.

In 1739, the baron Von Rosen wrote a letter to a high court in Livonia, in what became later known as "Rosen's Declaration." In this, he stated:

---

24. Smallpox similarly erased entire civilizations of mound-building Native Americans in the Southeastern United States, the ancestors of today's Choctaw and Creek tribes.

"Firstly, the nobility's dominion over the peasant dates to the time when this land was conquered [sic]. When the order of the German knights conquered this province with their spear, the peasant naturally lost his freedom and was reduced from a free member of society to one indentured [sic]... Peasants, including their bodies and consciousness, are now totally subject to their masters and belong to him... That which a peasant obtains, he does not earn for himself, but for his master. Therefore, the master has the right to manage his peasants' belongings as if they were his own... However, the nobility has softened these unlimited rights over the peasant and asks from them only tribute and corvee, leaving the rest to the peasant to encourage his diligence... These adjustments were never forced upon us by a government, but have always been of the nobility's free will, as evidenced by the Privileges of Sigismund Augustus" (Dunsdorfs, 1973, pg. 62).

Rosen's Declaration referenced the apocryphal Privilege of Sigismund Augustus, a King of Poland who supposedly guaranteed the Livonian nobility unlimited dominion over the peasants in 1561 after Tsar Ivan the Terrible invaded Livonia. Despite its repetition by Baltic Germans throughout Latvia's history in the Russian Empire, however, the document was either lost very early in its existence or it never existed at all, as nobody could produce it when prompted to.

Contrary to Von Rosen's assertions (and the now-nationally sacred narratives of Lāčplēsis and Gaismas Pils), as previously stated, the arrival of the Northern crusaders in Livonia affected indigenous lifestyle very little. After formally adopting Christianity, the Baltic and Finnic-speaking chieftains received their dominions back from the bishop as "fiefs," whilst continuing to govern and trade. Baltic peoples continued to sacrifice offerings to pagan gods in their sacred forest groves, and the chieftains only gradually Germanized over centuries or were replaced by ethnic Germans when falling in wars. Some indigenous, Latvian-speaking nobles even persisted unto modern day (the "Kings of Courland" – kuršu ķoniņi). Overall, the Livonian Confederation's legacy was thus to consolidate disparate tribes into 'two' Latvian and Estonian nations and spare them the Russification occurring to Balts and Finns living further east. Furthermore, until the late 1400's, corvee was also almost non-existent in Livonia (this role was filled by prisoners captured in war), and the institutionalized exclusion of Latvians from owning private property only arrived under the Russian scepter in 1710.

In 1561, Tsar Ivan the Terrible invaded Livonia, starting the Livonian War and dissolving the Livonian Confederation. The dueling Swedish and Polish Empires swept in to block Russia from accessing the sea and waged thirty more years of war between themselves for Baltic hegemony. During the 17th century, the Swedish Empire nationalized its private estates to better fund   an over-extended military. As a result of a Swedish ploughshare review, these nationalized 'crown estates' composed the bulk of plantations in Livonia and Estonia, providing a more productive and reliable tax base than private ones.

In addition to higher productivity, Swedish crown estates featured more humane conditions, and guaranteed rights to Latvians and Estonians that were unthinkable in the Russian Baltic a century later. Under Sweden, the Latvian peasant owned and took pride in maintaining his generational home, building personal wealth through his diligent labor. By contrast, during the 18th century, the Russian Empire's agrarian conditions inspired Pastor Hupel to write about Livonia: "Here, the people aren't as expensive as negroes in the American colonies"[25] (Dunsdorfs, 1973, pg. 76). Seeing the more scholarly historian's, Dunsdorfs', citation, we discern the racist bias present in Ģērmanis' own misquote of Hupel.

After the Great Northern War and plague of 1710, three decades passed for Baltic society to recuperate from Armageddon. To avoid exacerbating an already acute labor shortage, barons harkened to their "restored" privileges of Sigismund Augustus by tethering every peasant to a landowner in an otherwise unresolvable labor shortage. Debt bondage became institutionalized, and in the 18th century, the Latvian or Estonian languages became equated with servitude through prejudice and association. Baltic Germans even expected corvee from free yeomen (brīvzemnieki) if they spoke a language other than German.[26]

With a peasant's access to arable land contingent on giving corvee as rent, the landlords dispatched them to harvest grain and timber for vodka distilleries, which reaped obscene profits. Baltic Germans supplemented their income by fattening cattle from the Volga, Kalmykia, and Ukrainian steppes using their spent distillery grain. As a result of the vodka trade, Baltic Germans amassed fortunes.

---

25. "Ļaudis šeit nav tik dārgi kā nēģeri Amerikas kolonijās", which is subtly but significantly different from "Here, people are cheaper than negroes in America."
26. So noxious was 18th century serfdom in Livonia, that a foreigner's physical presence there imperiled his personal freedom. To travel the Livonian countryside, one required a passport for official business, otherwise opportunist barons might arrest this "runaway serf". To illustrate, we recall the fate of a battalion of Finnish soldiers in Livonia. During the 1600's, the Swedish crown stationed this battalion in northern Latvia to deter Polish incursion after three decades of warfare. Swedish law cyclically announced that these soldiers could not be enthralled as serfs, no matter how much debt they drew from a local creditor. After the Swedish defeat in the Great Northern War, however, the Baltic Germans refused to lease land to these former soldiers without receiving corvee as rent. Like Latvian and Estonian peasants, the soldiers sank into debt bondage, and after only a few generations, had assimilated fully into the Latvian and Estonian-speaking masses.

Whereas during Swedish times, noble "estates" often qualified as no more than peasant shacks with an extra room or two, under Russian rule, the nobility constructed palaces across Latvia and Estonia to rival the Antebellum South. Following the principle of 'more money, more problems' immortalized in black American culture, the Baltic German nobility naturally incurred gambling debt, which demanded still more corvee to cover. As a result, the Latvian peasantry worked 12 or more hours per day for decades, sometimes without adequate nutrition, facing physical abuse, eviction, or starvation should they strike.

All the stereotypes of Latvians depicted in Die Letten thus originated in the 1700s. Endemic violence was the result of chronic malnutrition and sleep deprivation. Petty theft was a natural response to poverty, and laziness was the result of institutional exclusion from personal or generational wealth. As the local adage went: "food was scarce, and alcohol was cheap."

In the 1700s Russian Baltic, aside from corporal punishment, religion was a favored method for restraining the brutalized and domesticated labor force. As part of the separate peace of 1710, the Baltic German nobility bargained for their "patron's rights" (patronātu tiesības) to select each parish's pastor. The Baltic Germans knew that a good religious leader was someone loyal to noble interests, and someone who functioned as a mouthpiece and surveillance system. This Lutheran church in Latvia and Estonia (kunga baznīca – the master's church) thus shroud noble directives as quasi-moral and religious ones, ceaselessly likening the baron's relationship with the peasant to that of Jesus Christ shepherding his flock.

Every Sunday, the Lutheran Church in Latvia advertised the social hierarchy through its seating arrangement. The 'patron' always occupied the first pew, along with other ethnic Germans and intellectuals behind. The subservient Latvians occupied the rear of the church, with the poorest relegated to the aisles, near the door, or listening from outside. Attendance was mandatory, if not always enforceable. Sermons emphasized the divine rewards awaiting the submissive and obedient, while threatening hellfire for the disobedient and lazy.

Lutheran burial practices further reinforced the ethno-class hierarchy. Burial in the church's hallowed cemetery signified a peasant's acceptance into Heaven, while exclusion from burial meant denial of salvation and the afterlife. The most disgraced peasants had their bodies flung into swamps as a symbol of eternal obliteration. Regardless of the crimes justifying a peasant's exclusion from burial (suicide was considered one because it stripped the baron of his labor force), the conduct of Lutheran ministers was often more disgraceful than of any peasant.

In 1733, the pastor of the town of Kalsnava and a graduate of Wittenberg Theological Seminary in Germany, "was fired for ongoing and open fornication, raping a maiden, corruption, and arriving to church each Sunday evening after brewing beer all day at home" (Johansons, 1975, pg. 256). In the first fifty years since the Great Northern War, thirty pastors were sanctioned or fired for crimes and coarse behavior. Their list of sins was long: sex-binges and other flouts to their duties of office; exploitation and manipulation of peasants (the most serious example being the 1746 trial of the pastor of Limbaži, who installed a whipping pole in his apartment); binge-drinking, alone or in company of church custodians, including one instance when they consumed all the church's wine. The pastor of Ropaži was sanctioned for constantly swearing during church service; at Eucharist, he denounced the members of his congregation as "God-damned devils," and defended his actions afterward with the excuse that his profanity 'only referenced the Bible' (Johansons, 1975, pg. 257).

But perhaps the most egregious crime of the Lutheran church in Livonia was also the most fundamental purpose- to remind Latvians and Estonians of their inferiority to Germans. Aside from physical segregation in the church nave according to class, a disobedient peasant could be made to sit for the entire service on the altar's so-called "stool of shame." Ministers read litanies of disobedient peasants that week on the estate, alongside their offenses and expected penances. As a result, the Latvian remained spiritually alienated from the faith; a Latvian miller once remarked that his pastor preaching was as insignificant to him as 'a barking dog.' Pastor Lange of Smiltene summarized Latvian attitudes toward spirituality in his 1750's journal:

"Regarding the problem of an Everlasting Life and the Undying Soul, the Latvian demonstrates a brutal and heroic indifference. When asked his overall thoughts about life or death, the Latvian replies: 'Here is another hard day, more threshing to be done, while there in the ground is a comfortable bed.'"

"The greatest pleasure in life for a Latvian," Pastor Lange wrote, "is to wrap himself in a warm sheepskin and sleep undisturbed behind the hearth... The Latvian cannot comprehend the Holy Scriptures' teachings of obedience to one's master, as he is unable to reconcile God's righteousness with his own suffocating yoke. For that same reason, the Latvian has no inkling of the grateful obedience a child owes his father, or that between a vassal and lord, between man and God" (Johansons, 1975, pg. 268).

The Lutheran church of Latvia continued to uphold class and ethnic prejudice until the first rifle shots of World War I. Thus, in contrast to the piety of the Latvian Catholic, the obtuse Latvian Lutheran could be summarized through the following anecdote:

"General Inquisitor Fischer was sent to Rūjiena [a mixed Latvian/ Estonian town in today's northern Latvia] where addressed the congregation from the pulpit.

"General inquisitor Fischer: "Who do you worship when you say the words "Our Father?"

"Answer from Latvians in the first pew: "God only knows!"

"Fischer: "Is it your own father, the one in the threshing barn, you worship when you say, "Our Father?""

"Latvians: "Yes."

"Fischer: "How can it be your father in the threshing barn, when you say, "Our Father, who art in Heaven?"

"Latvians: "God only knows!"

"Fischer repeated this same question to each member of the congregation, every one of them replying the same- "God only knows!" When he had finished, General Inquisitor Fischer clasped his hands behind his back and spoke from the altar: "This is a blindness one can only marvel at"" (Johansons, 1975, pg. 265).

In the 1730s, the Baltic Germans of Livonia reported the first mass defection of peasants to a new Protestant sect in the region, the Moravian Church. Despite the suddenly empty pews and collection plates on Sundays, not even the rapacious Baltic German ministers could rebuke the Moravian-converts' reformed morals. One pastor remarked how converted Latvians no longer sang their "vulgar shepherd songs" but instead wailed and lamented their sins from the meadows: "If God can awaken Abraham's children from rocks, then he can awaken schoolteachers within the Latvians" (Johansons, 1975, pg. 274-75) Converts to the Moravian Church rushed toward literacy, so that through only a few years of their influence, 60% of Latvian converts could already read.

A nominal sect of the Lutheran Church, the Moravian Church was initially expelled from Bohemia by Catholics during the Reformation. In 1727, a sympathetic count in Saxony sheltered the Moravians before financing their evangelism to the Baltics. The sect took root in Valmiera, a city in northern Latvia, from where it spread to the Latvian and Estonian countryside nearby.

Until this time, the stereotypical Latvian gazed upon foreigners with derision. The Latvian might ridicule the stranger for his accent, clothing, or manners. If the stranger knew enough broken Latvian to ask a question, then the Latvian peasant would either give a deliberate wrong answer or ignore the question altogether. Despite the Latvian's initial response to missionaries in this spirit, the Moravians breached the peasant's armor with their persistence and compassion. They approached Latvian peasants without class prejudice or arrogance; one surprised Latvian peasant even likened the first missionary's kindness to that of the Holy Savior.

In contrast to the socially segregated pews of the master's Lutheran church, Moravian congregations seated their parishioners in a benevolent circle. Instead of preaching in German or Latin, the Moravians proclaimed the Gospel in Latvian and ordered Bibles translated to Latvian imported from Saxony. At last able to comprehend the Bible's parables, the Latvian peasant finally integrated them into his behavior.

After the Moravian missionary's kindness, Latvian converts arrived for corvee each day the earliest of anyone, also working harder than anyone on the estate. Instead of drunkenness and boorishness, Latvian converts worshipped "with heretofore unseen fervor." Whereas a Latvian might once summarize a German-language parable with a yawn and say, "that was a good story" (tā bija laba pasaka), as a Moravian convert, he practiced preaching the Gospel himself from the hayfields. Theft or misappropriation of estate property ceased altogether.

Within a decade, literacy amongst the Latvian and Estonian peasants began its trajectory toward amongst the highest in the Russian Empire. Eager to decipher more Biblical passages, hymns, and treatises, peasants congregated at Moravian home-schools for reading lessons. A century before becoming one of the Russian Empire's most literate ethnicity, the Latvian began his journey to literacy by drawing letters into the dirt with sticks. Once he'd practiced that, he practiced writing his sins as a form of penance, keeping journals, and exchanging letters. Education and literacy led to improved record-keeping and increased prosperity.

In contrast to illiterate and uneducated peasants, who enriched the estate taverns by spending all their spare cash on vodka, the Moravian converts donated their surplus monies to construct a chapel. This gathering place – "Jēra Kalns," the Lamb's Hill – seated 1,000 members on wooden benches encircling the pulpit. Light streamed in through six glass windows, while a clay hearth heated the chapel in winter. During evening services or the notoriously long nights of December and January, chandeliers bathed the chapel in candlelight and allowed parishioners to read the Gospel year-round.

By 1740, the number of "awakened" Moravian converts in Livonia approached 5,000 (Johansons, 1975, pg. 276). Despite the increased productivity of peasant corvee and decreased workplace theft on the estates, the Baltic Germans gazed upon the Moravian Church with scorn and jealousy. Rather than celebrating a productive labor force, conservative Baltic Germans sensed only an erosion of their authority; Lutheran ministers preached to suddenly empty pews, and weekly collection plates weighed less and less.

In 1742, enough Baltic Germans launched complaints against the Moravian Church that they forced the provincial government to investigate. By performing 'illegal' Baptisms and weddings, the Baltic nobility argued, the Moravian Church had "stolen privileges" belonging solely to the establishment per the concessions of Tsar Peter in 1710. And despite the egalitarian division of Moravian responsibilities, the Baltic Germans accused the "sect" of electing incompetent Latvians to religious office. Indeed, according to Moravian traditions, Latvians sometimes cast lots to pick candidates according to "God's will". Sometimes, also, the most fanatical peasants claimed to be the Apostle Paul incarnate.

In 1743, the Tsarina Elizabeth I issued an official decree outlawing the Moravian Church in the Russian Empire. "Secret diplomacy" from Baltic Germans in the imperial court undoubtedly influenced her decision. Repression of the Moravian Church began immediately; police boarded up Jēra Kalns, collected and burned Moravian archives, and forced the Brotherhood's leadership underground. By 1750, the chapel at Jēra Kalns was demolished.

Despite the repression, the Moravian Church continued to exist underground like a smoldering, Latvian bog fire. The prohibition trained Brothers to avoid scrutiny and to subvert repression by denouncing the movement publicly while supporting it privately. Latvian converts held religious services aboard rafts on the Gauja river in Valmiera. Historian Johansons draws a direct link from Moravian centers of the 1730s to the peasant uprising in the later 18th century: "The Moravian Brotherhood unwittingly reared Latvian peasants into becoming active fighters against the nobility" (Johansons, 1975, pg. 287).

Just as black soldiers of the 20th century refused to return to segregation in America after returning from abroad (Wilkerson, 2020, pg. 227), literate Latvian peasants could no longer exist as mindless livestock. The labor strikes and armed insurrections of the 18th century exploded most ferociously in areas of Moravian influence. In contrast to the Latvian Americans I witnessed decrying "burning and looting" after George Floyd's murder in 2020, these uprisings burned and looted Baltic German private property for 70 years until forcing serfdom's first repeal in 1819.

Long after the Moravian Church introduced the Latvian peasantry to literacy, however, Baltic German barons continued trafficking their Latvian serfs. Editions of the German-language newspaper Rigische Anzeigen published for-sale and wanted-ads, as well as notices of runaway peasants that the literate runaways could now sometimes decipher. Indicative that the conflict in the Russian Baltic was still somewhere between a class and an ethnic one, Johansons remarks that other ethnicities besides Latvians could become serfs. "Not only Latvians, but Estonians and Russians were also traded at the market. In 1769, a German woman was even advertised, along with her four-year-old child. For a separate price, the buyer could obtain the child individually" (Johansons, 1975, pg. 70).

In 1771, the Russian Imperial Senate finally banned selling peasants at live auction, but such a powerful lobby existed in the Baltic, that the law's publication was suppressed until 1789. Advertisements highlighted one Latvian weaver's "pleasant disposition, good health, no issues with alcohol, and ability to weave the most complicated patterns." Often, the price of a Latvian peasant was decided "upon agreement", but otherwise, the price was simply noted as being "low" (Johansons, 1975, pg. 70).

Like the flight of slaves before the Civil War, like the six million black Americans who emigrated from the Jim Crow South, the most realistic escape for many Latvian peasants was often to simply flee. This form of passive protest produced such a labor shortage in Livonia, that it repeatedly demanded investigation from the Imperial government. One analysis in 1765 found that "unrestricted noble power, tax burden and corvee, which not only exceeded that of neighboring lands, but also the limits of humanity," drove peasants from their homes. As early as 1719, Livonian barons could legally brand "shame symbols" into the faces of captured runaways; others maintained their authority by threatening to sell the sons of disobedient peasants to the army.[27]

_____

27. Maintaining dominance was a matter of honor for the Baltic Ger- mans as much as an economic one. A newspaper in 1795 described one runaway cook as having "no faults, other than his freedom-mania," and promised three hundred silver rubles for his return. The advertisement announced that if whoever cap-tured the cook wished to retain him, he could be purchased on the condition of never receiving freedom from his new master. "May he remain a chamber servant wherever he may reside." Thus, to be a Latvian in the 18th century meant being nothing more than a servant (Merķelis, 2016, pg. 75).

If passive protest meant emigration, then active protest first meant filing lawsuits in parish courts, followed by labor strikes and rebellion. With the ability to read and write now secured from Moravian missionaries, from the 1740s to the 1760s, Latvian peasants filed flurries of lawsuits against their masters in parish courts regarding excessive corvee or corporal punishment. Just as the nobility selected parish ministers, they also elected local police and juries, stacking Livonian social institutions in their favor. Because of this, the accusations were often rejected, and the barons retaliated at home with yet more whippings.

Widespread Latvian peasant labor strikes erupted in 1771, 1776, 1784, and 1802, although localized instances of unrest occurred nearly every year at least somewhere in Livonia or Estonia. In Die Letten, Garlieb Merkel wrote that mere rumors of foreign invasion drove the Baltic nobles to hide their valuables and bury their treasures. In the event of a real invasion, Garlieb Merkel stated, they knew the Latvian peasants would avenge the "long-broken social contract" like the black Haitians did in 1804.[28]

After a particularly stinging lawsuit loss in 1765 with a poor harvest in 1770, the peasantry of Livonia was especially embittered and primed for rebellion. In 1771, rumors of an approaching Polish force spurred these peasants to storm a local estate, disarm the local police there, and loot and vandalize the palace. They also refused to give corvee for the rest of the season as they awaited

28. Nonetheless, the attitude of local, conservative authorities toward the Enlightenment appears in the writings of Baltic governors: "What a misfortune to live in this era, when people philosophize so much about 'rights,' and when all of Europe is inflamed with this chimeric plague of 'freedom'" (Švābe, 1958, pg. 69). Another baron, Woldemar von Ungern- Sternberg, writes: "These Enlightenment thinkers, who incite civil war, need to all be hung. And the people that follow this nonsense because it is fashionable need to be sent back to school and re-educated."

their Polish 'liberators.' Although no Polish army ever materialized, the rebellion spread to surrounding estates, and soon exceeded the capacity of local police. After several weeks of chaos, the Livonian general governor dispatched the military to quell the disorder.

In 1776, future tsar Paul I crossed Livonia in his carriage. When Livonian peasants learned of his journey, they gathered from multiple estates in Valmiera county, the center of the Moravian movement, and swarmed the carriage to complain about unjust rulings by parish courts. When Paul I's entourage accepted the complaints for further investigation, the Baltic German nobility blocked their motion as "legally unprecedented." Like Republicans filing audits against the apocryphal ballot fraud of the 2020 presidential election in the United States, the local Baltic courts investigated those Latvians who dared to appeal for justice.

Soon enough, the peasants who'd swarmed the imperial carriage refused to serve one baron in particular, Carl Adam Wulf.[29] Left unsatisfied after their demands for an investigation into his sadism were ignored, 72 peasants signed a memorandum demanding permanent emancipation from him. As a matter of prestige, the investigative committee rebuked such 'radical' demands; rather, in their reply, they reminded Latvian peasants about the 'sanctity' of private property before they initiated mass arrests.[30]

---

29 . Wulf's list of sins was long. In addition to sadistic levels of corvee and exploitation, Baron Wulf was investigated, tried, and convicted for striking a pregnant Latvian woman. Though convicted, Baron Wulf's punishment was a mere seventy-five daalder fine to the Livonian nobility's corporation and to reduce taxes for his peasants for three years.

30. The peasants were instructed that the estates were purchased for good money, and that for this money, the barons retained the rights to use the peasantry however needed. Should the peasant refuse to comply with noble directives, the committee argued, then he ought to repay the mortgage himself. "Look how idiotic your reasoning is. Will the Tsarina herself come here to judge this matter? Who would let such pigs as you near the Empress?" (Dunsdorfs, 1973, pg. 89)

At this time, the peasants and the government reached an impasse. Without traction in the local courts, peasants continued insisting on direct negotiation with Tsarina Catherine herself. Summarily, the Baltic German courts sentenced the peasants to public flogging for their intransigence. Two thousand local Latvians were herded together before the main church of Valmiera to observe the punishment, with some ordered to administer the first strikes. Just as the first blows were delivered, the Latvian onlookers began hurling bricks and rocks at the police, and a military guard was needed to disperse the crowd and protect the court and nobility. After the unrest of 1776, Baltic German nobles attributed a new stereotype to Latvian peasants: mutinous and disobedient by nature, they were unable to forgo their "freedom sickness"[31] (Dunsdorfs, 1973, pg. 91).

The most serious and widespread Latvian peasant uprising occurred from 1783 to 1784, the so-called Poll-Tax Uprisings (Galvasnaudas Nemieri). During her reign, Tsarina Catherine the Great instituted policies curtailing Baltic autonomy and regulating tax collection; to simplify taxation, she instituted a poll tax of 70 kopeks per household to be collected by the nobles and passed along to the crown.

From the outset, this poll tax was vulnerable to abuse; as the Baltic Germans paid the crown in cash directly, they greatly inflated the Latvian peasant's corvee and tribute while pocketing the difference without the peasant's knowledge. A single ambiguous sermon convinced some Latvian peasants that anyone who paid his poll tax directly to the Tsarina was liberated of duties to the Baltic German. Chronically malnourished, sleep-deprived, and perpetually hungover,

---

31. Freiheitstriebe

the Latvian peasants latched onto this rumor with infectious fervor. Thus, a single, unfounded rumor of liberation exploded from one parish to another.

Peasants in Valmiera County, the epicenter of the Moravian Church four decades earlier, organized labor strikes once again and refused to work until they were allowed to pay their poll tax without Baltic German intermediacy. An inconsistent government response across Livonia further emboldened the peasants. For instance, when some officials, but not others, refused to accept the poll tax directly from peasants, Latvians attacked their local courts and assaulted authorities.

Of course, missed corvee from a general labor strike threatened not only the nobility's profit margins, but also their authority. So instead of negotiating with an already starving and overworked peasantry, the nobles requested military assistance to suppress it. By September of 1784, the equivalent of one soldier to every household was deployed to Livonia, and when the dreaded, mounted Don-River Cossacks[32] arrived with their whips, the season's rebellion summarily extinguished.

Just as the Latvian fervor for communism smoldered despite suppression of the 1905 revolution, discontent amongst the Latvian peasants seethed long after the Poll Tax Uprising. In fact, annual unrest ensured that elite political discussions in the Baltic almost always circled around the "peasant question." Conservative defenders of serfdom merely voiced concerns about whether limiting human trafficking would impact their profitability. One baron even wrote: "A motion to restrict purchase or sale of peasants runs contrary

---

32. A mixed Ukrainian and Russian cavalry host hailing from southern Russia

to a free market. These restrictions only hamper competition and reduce their value" (Švābe, 1958, pg. 60).

In the 1790s, the Jacobin Terror overtook France just before Die Letten's publication, and word of the guillotine doubtlessly reached the Latvian peasantry without Garlieb Merkel's help. In 1802, another large uprising around Valmiera (again) forced local and imperial governments to finally reckon with indentured servitude. After three years of failed harvests (1799-1801), inter-class and inter-ethnic tensions had boiled over; Latvian peasants from Valmiera, Kauguri, Burtnieki, Rauna, and Cēsis (all towns within Moravian influence) began a concerted labor strike. During the summer of 1802, the nobility's rye and oats remained unharvested in the fields, while their hay and linen lodged and rotted. The labor strike incensed the Baltic Germans so much they demanded a military intervention from the imperial government at once.

In Kauguri, the Latvian peasants rallied with stakes and scythes against an artillery ordered to disperse them. After exchanging gunfire and succumbing to arrest, the captured strike leader, Gotarts Johansons, acknowledged reading his master's newspapers on a weekly basis including the news from France. Not only had Johansons admitted to reading contraband copies of Die Letten before the uprisings, but he'd also translated and disseminated chapters of this work amongst his fellow Latvians.

After the Kauguri Uprising of 1802, the tsar ordered an investigation into the uprising's cause, specifically with the intent of reforming Baltic living conditions and unrooting the perennial revolts. He deputized a Baltic German named Parrot, the rector of the University of Tartu and also an Enlightenment-sympathizer, to spearhead the project. Parrot's own investigation called for repealing human trafficking, 'the most heinous economy' in the Baltics.' Parrot wrote: "what good is frugality and diligence for him, who the baron can evict at a moment's notice and strip of his wife and children... Let us leave the baron what belongs to him- his property- but let us return to the peasant the fields he cultivates, for this is his holy right" (Švābe, 1958, pg. 71).

Ultimately, Parrot called for redistribution of the land as private property amongst the peasants. In 1803, a landtag convened in Livonia to discuss overhauling the Baltic's agrarian order. Since fear of federal interference sometimes motivated conservative nobles more than anything else, this landtag was unusually well attended. Amidst the chaos of a crowded, German-speaking hall, the nobility's conservative bloc summarized this 1803 reform project as "a few fools and beggars proposing to liberate the serfs... and with these Jacobin methods conquer the tsar's heart" (Švābe, 1958, pg. 73).

In the usual way, denunciations and intrigues emerged amongst the disgruntled nobility unwilling to surrender privilege. Regardless, the tsar overrode the landtag's veto, accepting a reform project that officially acknowledged the Latvian and Estonian peasants had been exploited. This ensuing Law of 1804 repealed indentured servitude and permitted peasants to choose their employer so long as they remained inside the county's borders (to prevent provincial labor shortage). Human trafficking of Latvian laborers was officially abolished, although the practice continued legally for personal and household servants. According to the Law of 1804, nobles could also no longer evict tenants for laziness or carelessness without a court order either.

Amidst the Napoleonic Wars, the Law of 1804 was thrown out and replaced with several other schemes. The famous "Land Surveys"

(Mērnieku Laiki) in the Baltic delineated peasant fields from estate property from 1809-1823. Serfdom was repealed de jure in the Baltic provinces from 1816-1819, five decades before the rest of the Russian Empire. Nonetheless, conservative Baltic Germans ensured a caveat; like the white Southerners who retained their plantations after the Civil War, which they might lease to black, landless sharecroppers in exchange for labor, the Baltic German nobility maintained total private ownership of the land. In this new agrarian order, the Latvian peasant received the following offer: The land is mine, the time is yours. To feed himself and his family by accessing the land, the Latvian farmer had to accept whatever terms and conditions the landlord wanted, all with a smile on his face.

The Early 19th Century in Colonial Latvia

In 1803, the Livonian landtag finally convened to write the first law of emancipation. According to this "Law of 1804," the peasants would no longer be bound to an estate, but received small plots from the estate to cultivate privately. The law intended to decriminalize the already common practice of fleeing an estate and leading to local labor shortage. The Law of 1804 also specifically applied only to 'ploughmen'— the heads of household; servants of the estates could still be trafficked at market, exchanged as gifts, advertised in newspapers, or inherited as property.

As is often the case when trying to "compromise" on divisive issues such as whether to pay your workforce or not, the Law of 1804 satisfied neither the peasantry nor the barons. In response to the law, a conservative, noble task force immediately proposed reclassifying every farmstead's plow and other iron equipment ("dzelzs inventārs") as estate property, so that the peasant could not cultivate their land without accepting the Baltic German's terms and conditions to lease the farm tools.

For peasants to receive private plots according to the 1804 Law, they furthermore required land surveys to evaluate and demark property's boundaries. Each plot also had to be appraised for a tax debt. The value of a plot considered not only its soil's fertility, but also the geographical proximity to roads, nearby infrastructure, and to markets. Peasant tax burdens were recorded into the "county booklets" (vaku grāmatas) and issued physically to each peasant to codify their obligations to the state. In theory, county booklets assured peasants against exploitation or extortion from corrupt landlords, but the local justice systems under noble payroll often flouted the county booklets.

Many Baltic German barons also bribed surveyors to increase the peasant tax debt through the land surveys taking place from 1809-1823. Bribe-taking surveyors over-valued sandy or swampy soil to boost a disfavored peasant's corvee. Other farces included classifying soil that could sustain a crop for only three consecutive years before laying fallow for two decades as "agricultural land," or inflating timber value to justify more corvee for vodka distillation.

Napoleon's advances disrupted the first implementation of 1804's reform. As Napoleon charged across Europe, the Russian government prepared for impending war by mobilizing its army and turning away from domestic oversight. During the surveys then, Baltic German barons could exploit the chaos by issuing flurries of bureaucratic notes to exhaust the overwhelmed Interior Ministry. With Napoleon storming eastward, first into German 'Prussia', then Poland, the over-litigated government shelved its oversight of the land surveys completely to concentrate on the impending war.

As Napoleon continued his advance, liberating serfs in one province after the next – Schleswig-Holstein (1805), Pomerania (1806), and East Prussia (1807)- the barons and the federal government settled their differences to avoid an uncontrolled repeal of serfdom. As the Russian Empire's western border depended on the conservative, Baltic nobles ("the knightage") to buttress against invaders, naturally, if these barons proclaimed their loyalty as they once did for Tsar Peter, then Russia would capitulate readily to their demands.

The Law of 1804 became the heavily mangled Law of 1809. County booklets from 1804 were invalidated, and precise land surveys were streamlined to averages– 1/2, ¼, 1/8 of a vaguely defined "ploughshare". Property borders shifted readily; in accordance with the surveys before 1809, the land surveyors had demarcated peasant plots using survey markers in nature, and red lines on maps. But without federal oversight, border falsification surged. Furthermore, barons often duped and intimidated peasants into financing estate construction projects during this time, citing 1809's "updates" to the law, despite construction projects traditionally having always been an estate expense.

Due to such discrepancy amongst the county booklets, the Latvian peasant rightfully avoided further dealings with them. Rumors floated from village to village like anti-vaccine propaganda: whoever accepts one of the new booklets will remain indentured; whoever refuses them becomes free. The Russian government, fully alert to Latvian skepticism regarding anything German, signed and stamped the Imperial eagle onto every booklet for legitimacy. Naturally, the tsar wanted to avoid defrauding the peasants also standing between Napoleon's troops and Moscow's gates.

In 1811, one year before Napoleon marched on Moscow, an official county booklet in Latvia containing the Imperial eagle displayed signs of forgery. Riots erupted in Sidgunda and Mālpils. When reformists suggested that only an entirely new land survey could re-legitimize the county booklets in the peasantry's eyes, the nobles reacted with typical conservative logic; a second land survey would set a "dangerous political precedent," whereby rebellion would be condoned and "only encourage future unrest" (Švābe, 1958, pg. 94). Therefore, instead of unrooting corruption and economic privilege, the Baltic German nobility accused Latvian peasants of inciting riots and sentenced them to 50 public lashings.

Although the Russians could halt Napoleon's troops by torching Moscow in 1812, they couldn't halt the spread of Enlightenment ideals accompanying him. Through Poland, where peasants had already habituated to Napoleon's emancipation, Tsar Aleksander inherited the legacy of serfdom's repeal in his empire without ever decreeing it. Recognizing that emancipation from serfdom was inevitable, the tsar declared the Baltic provinces his sandbox- from a safe distance, he could experiment here with emancipation while minimizing the labor shortages or production deficits in the Russian heartland.

In 1816, under Tsar Aleksander I's pressure, the provincial landtag of Estonia finally repealed serfdom across the province. In 1817, the nobility of Courland Province voted to follow Estonia's example, and in 1819, Livonia joined them. Despite having spent vast sums on now-pointless land surveys since 1809, the nobles of Livonia Province, in particular, joined their neighbors to the west and north by liberating the serfs de jure fifty years before the rest of the Russian Empire.

Three centuries after its introduction to Europe via the Columbian Exchange, the cultivation of the calorie-rich and hardy potato had barely touched the tables of Latvians by the 19th century. The reason: Latvians resisted all German 'improvements' to agriculture, seeing in them only opportunity for more exploitation. Indeed, while the high starch tuber thrived in boreal climates like in the Baltic, its usefulness as a reliable crop certainly wasn't wasted on feeding the peasantry. Two decades after their emancipation from serfdom, the Latvian peasantry sometimes even provided more hours of corvee than before emancipation; potatoes grown on the estates made superb distillable material for vodka, after all.

Since the repeal of serfdom, a farmstead worth 20 daalders still owed its landlord 700 workdays each year from both a laborer on horse (zirdzinieks, īstenieks) and another on foot (kājnieks) as rent. Functionally, this meant that four laborers per farmstead worked nearly every day of the year to process enough potatoes into vodka to satisfy their lease. But because estate jobs took **precedence** over personal crops, as soon as the summons to work at the distillery arrived each morning, the sowing and harvesting of personal crops awaited corvee's daily completion or rain days.

A century after the "classical" serfdom of the 1700s, the potato had made vodka **preferable** to food once again. A pastor in the city of Jelgava remarked that in his parish, there was "one church, six schools, and 66 taverns" (Švābe, 1958, pg. 181). Alcohol was cheaper than food and provided respite for the Latvian from his despair. In 1842, Baltic German barons from Livonia even exported 120,000 "buckets" of vodka to Petrograd, and 20,000 more to the Pskov governorate just east of Latvia and Estonia (Švābe, 1958). The spirits, made with unpaid labor, **reaped tremendous** profits. With these profits, the Baltic Germans raised manors and palaces mirroring Tara plantation from Gone with the Wind.

Frustrated by their persistent starvation, unrest seethed in 1831 as 278 Latvians peasants testified against their landlord in Cesvaine. They accused him of bankrupting them with his vodka-running caravans to Pskov and Vitebsk governorates and exhausting their draft horses to death (which they still needed to use to **fulfill other rent obligations**). Local police, the loyal guardians of private property across all ages and cultures, dispersed the gathering before conducting mass arrests resulting in death sentences. Just as the gallows in Cesvaine hung ready for their victims, a mob of several thousand Latvian peasants arrived brandishing pitchforks and clubs. The police halted the execution temporarily to discuss how to best proceed against a mob vastly **outnumbering** them.

Fearing nothing more than another federal intervention, a local tribunal reviewed the case in Cesvaine and ruled the baron there liable to recompense his peasants for their corvee exceeding the county booklets. However, a higher court controlled by the nobility managed to stall this ruling's enforcement until 1843, when the statute of limitations expired.

The summers of 1835-1837 were so uncharacteristically cold and rainy that they yielded grain and potatoes rotting in the mud. During the cold autumns that followed, winter rye failed to germinate. Additionally, since the 'emancipation,' the Baltic Germans had exempted themselves from any public granary upkeep or welfare. With so many consecutive failed harvests, starving Latvians grasped out for any rumors offering respite from their wretched lives. After witnessing several hundred Jewish families emigrate to maritime Ukraine near Kherson, rumors swelled amongst the Latvians that the tsar was giving away land in his vast empire, specifically an area the Latvians called "warm lands."

In 1841, members of the Latvian and Estonian peasantry became the first "warm lands" enthusiasts to emigrate. Initially, when crossing the provincial borders southbound to Lithuania, the border guards simply denied the peasants entry and forced them to return home. The harshness of apprehensions accelerated, however, when the Baltic German nobles started noticing labor defections. "The police of Rīga began arresting rural countrymen who arrived to obtain travel passports. The arrested were then publicly flogged before the general governor's mansion, and some had their heads half-shaven like heavy criminals at the time" (Švābe, 1958, pg. 193).

Disillusioned, the peasants returned to their farmsteads but refused to pay rent or provide corvee. By mid-September, flashpoints erupted in both Estonia (Pühajärve) and in Latvia (Jaunbebri), where professional police battalions collided with Latvian peasants brandishing pitchforks, scythes, and pikes.

In Jaunbebri, the local baron Tranze ordered his estate police to arrest any potato diggers refusing to work. Brandishing their stakes and pitchforks, the Latvians repelled the battalion, who retreated to Tranze's estate. As the policemen sheltered inside, the peasant laborers surrounded the manor, demanding Baron Tranze appear for negotiations. The peasants' siege lasted several days, before two companies of soldiers arrived and scattered the insurgents. In all, the peasantry had intimidated Tranze enough to order five military companies and 40 Cossacks as reinforcements, along with two artillery pieces.

A bureaucratic investigation into the events at Jaunbebri and the so-called "Warm Lands Movement" blamed the Lutheran Church for inciting Latvian and Estonian peasants to emigrate. Although from the pulpit, the clergy still preached the Gospel of Baltic German supremacy, in private, some criticized the nobility for its cruel, agrarian politics. In 1841, the Lutheran Synod of Livonia declared: "The peasants openly affirm that after emancipation, they have lost all interest in maintaining their farmsteads, hopeless as they are as tenants without rights to the property for their children or descendants. Wherever the county booklets mention regulating corvee, it is disproportionately high compared to the farmstead's true value; now the corvee is unbearable, and heads of household become responsible for local county taxes as well as money to hire assistants to keep up with housework. The demands of the manorial economy greatly exceed anything the peasants can deliver, especially during sowing and the harvest" (Švābe, 1958, pg. 195).

The Latvian labor strikes at Jaunbebri further exposed the rift between the nobility and the Lutheran clergy. When the nobility stabbed back at the clergy by officially denouncing the Lutheran church for causing the Warm Lands Movement, the clergy retorted that the contrast between the peasantry's endemic poverty with noble palaces proved the selfishness of the Baltic agrarian order.

As the constant peasant refrain of the era was: "we no longer wish to obey the barons, we are loyal to only God and the Tsar," the Baltic German clergy and nobles finally reconciled their differences by condemning the Russian Orthodox Church for the whole mess. Evidently, the tsar respected the investigative committees of Baltic Germans more than to his own peasant subjects, as he ordered all Orthodox priests henceforth to cease interactions with Lutheran Latvian or Estonian peasants.

Punitive expeditions for the Warm Lands Uprising commenced in December 1841 with the traditional military punishment of driving the accused through rows of 300 or more soldiers. As the accused ran, each soldier struck out with a switch or a leather belt to flog the victim. In Pühajärve, Estonia and in Jaunbebri, Latvia, officers with chalk in hand marked the helmets of soldiers they believed failing to strike the peasant with enough force; these guilty soldiers were then flogged themselves. 30 Estonian peasants at Pühajärve received 15,000 floggings between themselves, while in Jaunbebri, the same fate befell 113 Latvian peasants (Švābe, 1958). Of the accused insurgents, teenagers were beaten as savagely as adults, and elderly women received up to 100 whippings. Flesh tumbled off the bone. Whoever fainted during the punishment was tied to a sled and dragged alongside another row of whippings until they died. Those that survived the floggings spent their lives in prison or exile to Siberia.

To an assembly of peasants gathered and forced to observe the punishments, a judge remarked: "This is how we treat those who wish to depart for 'warmer lands.' This is how we treat whoever gets the idea to convert to the Russian faith, and whoever disobeys their master and minister!" (Švābe, 1958, pg. 197) After the brutality at Jaunbebri, the drive to peacefully emigrate 'to warmer lands' amongst Latvians evaporated.

After the fallout of the "Warm Lands Movement" and its savage punitive expeditions, even the most conservative members of the nobility reassessed their relations to the Latvian peasant. The Baron Georg Nolken, once a vocal proponent of the "German's historical mission" to civilize the Baltic, wrote: "The chasm between the nobility and peasantry is as sharp today as it was six hundred years ago [sic]. Even now, the peasant gazes at the baron as a foreign invader, who forcefully deprived him of his land and illegally holds it. The peasant of Livonia has never recognized the legitimacy of large landholders here. The peasant continues to assert his rights to the land" (Švābe, 1958, pg. 197).

Although Nolken similarly misconstrued the history of the Northern Crusades and Livonian Confederation, his summary shows how deeply these myths reverberated across social classes of the Baltic since the Great Plague of 1711.

Following the first, failed attempts at peaceful emigration from the Baltic, as the next failed act of peaceful protest, Latvian peasants defected in mass from Lutheranism to Russian Orthodoxy. The converts rarely adopted Orthodox customs, remaining entirely indifferent to dogma. Instead, converted Latvians mostly emphasized now belonging "only to God and the tsar" in hopes of winning tsarist favor and intervention in their struggle. After the first congregation in Riga received the title "Latvian Orthodox" in 1840, the number of converts in Livonia Province (with mixed Latvian and Estonian populations) grew to 113,000 in 10 years, or 12% of the populace (Švābe, 1958, pg. 209).

In 1840, a Moravian Church minister named Dāvis Balodis began preaching the movement's tenets to factory workers in Riga. When the highest Lutheran authority of Riga forbade Balodis from continuing to profess this doctrine, Balodis sought patronage from a Russian Orthodox bishop. After promising to nominally convert his congregation to Orthodoxy, Balodis received a space to continue services, preaching in the Latvian language and singing traditional Lutheran hymns for liturgy. This chimeric denomination soon radiated to the rest of Livonia.

The 1840s wave of conversions was not a spiritual awakening, but a political statement. The Latvian peasantry and Orthodox fathers alike helped disseminate rumors that the tsar was granting free land in his vast Empire to anyone adopting Orthodoxy. While these rumors were entirely baseless, the rumors insisted nonetheless that the tsar's will was being deliberately "hidden." Services of the Latvian Orthodox church also betrayed its political motives; Latvian services never adopted Orthodox customs like adoration of icons, fasting, or the Orthodox direction of signing the cross. Instead, Latvian Orthodoxy continued traditions from Lutheranism such as a focus on the minister's sermon, Gospel songs, and devotion to Biblical passages.

Such a massive and abrupt defection to Orthodoxy as 50,000 parishioners in 1847 alone (Švābe, 1958, pg. 209) startled both the Baltic German nobles and the federal government. Barons reacted by threatening Latvian Orthodox peasants with eviction or exclusion from traditional sacraments (remember that exclusion from funerals meant exclusion from the afterlife). They also rewarded loyal Lutheran Latvians with better farmsteads and labor contracts. The tsarist government, meanwhile, eager to accelerate the pace of ethnic assimilation across the empire, announced in 1849 that all Estonian and Latvian converts were legally obliged to henceforth worship in the Russian language. Converted Latvians, already facing pressure from the Baltic Germans, now faced deportation to Siberia for rejecting a language foreign to them. Orthodox Latvians trying to baptize their children back into Lutheranism faced child custody loss.

The rumors and hopes of land, liberation from corvee, and tsarist favor all proved illusional; for their peaceful protest, Latvian and Estonian converts received neither land nor freedom. Embittered, from 1853-1860, a few more Latvian converts travelled by horse and carriage to the Black Sea, where they participated in founding the modern Russian city of Yeysk by the Azov.

Witnessing the "Warm Lands Movement" and the mass Latvian defection to Russian Orthodoxy, a young, liberal Baltic German named Hamilcar von Fölkersahm returned to the Baltic from his studies in Berlin. Eager to make practical use of his academic knowledge, in 1838, Fölkersahm purchased an estate in northern Latvia and officially joined the Livonian landtag as a newly landed noble. For the next three years, Fölkersahm parsed Livonia's Emancipation Act of 1819, coming to terms with his own ethnicity's economic privilege and domination of the Baltic's indigenous people. Fölkersahm publicly compared Livonia's 1819 repeal of serfdom to a German noble "outstretching his hand to grab the fruit of another" (Švābe, 1958, pg. 198).

Attending landtag conferences, Fölkersahm persuaded some Baltic German delegates to join his "agroliberal" faction. Leading this faction, Fölkersahm proposed an entirely new agrarian order for Livonia- one giving Latvian and Estonians private property ownership and replacing their debt-labor with cash payments to the estates. To justify this, Fölkersahm harkened to an existential threat for Baltic Germans; in 30 years' time, a quota of land must be sold to small Latvian and Estonian landholders, or else the Baltic Germans risked a catastrophic peasant uprising like the one foretold by Garlieb Merkel five decades earlier.

Dismissing Fölkersahm, the conservative nobles equated all reforms with an attack on German identity the way Republican opponents lance Critical Race Theory today. They likened hungry Latvians with spoiled children: "No reforms are necessary – they will only reinforce the peasant into thinking he can get everything he wants through unrest. The fault is not within the nobility, but in the character of the peasant, who loves nothing, becomes attached to nothing, and only seeks thrill and novelty in strange places" (Švābe, 1958, pg. 200).

Although the conservatives considered a perceived loss of privilege to be a fatal issue for them, Fölkersahm had already persuaded his liberal supporters to adopt an amendment to the Act of 1819. The amendment included a ban on stacking corvee days from the winter to the summer, a prohibition on ordering peasants to cultivate vodka potatoes among their personal gardens, and a cap of twelve-hour workdays. These "22 points" went to the tsar for approval, who ratified them. However, conservative barons demanded that even these meager reforms be kept secret, never announced in print or official edict, but by Lutheran pastors at their parish sermons. The goal of downplaying reform was to prevent "rewarding" the peasants for their "bad behavior" of revolt. Many barons furthermore endeavored to misinform their workers of the new law and legal rights as much as possible.

Ultimately, conservative Baltic Germans managed to hijack Fölkersahm's reform project in 1842 by unraveling its implementation. Using fear and intimidation, they convinced the liberal faction that "doing nothing at all" would somehow prevent unrest better than fulfilling a meaningful reform. A disillusioned Fölkersahm left for sabbatical in Berlin to reevaluate his methods and motives, leaving the Latvians and Estonians without their charismatic ally in the landtag.

With over 600 peasant uprisings occurring across Russia under the thirty-year reign of Tsar Nikolai I (1825-1855), the imperial government readily experimented with reform to neutralize these disruptions. Not forgetting the nobility's role in repelling Napoleon a few decades before, the tsar balanced the wellbeing of the peasantry, upon which Russia depended for agricultural output, with the conservative nobility's boundless greed. In 1846, the tsar finally granted an audience to the Baltic German representatives from the Baltic, where he announced that the Emancipation Acts of 1819 had clearly failed; despite 'emancipation,' peasant unrest was still roiling the countryside after three decades.

The mass defection of Latvians from Lutheranism to Russian Orthodoxy, the tsar explained, could be understood only as the fruit of the Lutheran clergy's own negligence and hypocrisy. Indeed, since the Great Northern War, Lutheran clergymen had managed their own palaces using money from the collection plates, profiteering in vodka distillation just as the barons with corvee, all while under the guise of "serving Christ." When the baron G. Meiendorf defended the clergy of Livonia Province, the tsar queried him as to why mass conversion hadn't also occurred in Finland or elsewhere containing Lutheran minorities, but in Livonia province alone. Without waiting for an answer, the tsar insisted that a need for federal intervention had arisen.

Imperially-initiated reform conferences resumed in Livonia, where Russian Orthodox ministers insisted the Land Surveys had artificially inflated property values and undervalued corresponding corvee. This, of course, was the result of rampant "administrative expenses"[33] by the nobility. Latvian and Estonian peasants, the Orthodox fathers said, worked harder and for less value than even the most backward peasants of the Russian Empire's heartland. However, the Baltic Germans immediately dismissed this talk of impoverished peasantry as a red herring, silently disturbed that their costly bribes during the land surveys had produced such inaccurate results.

Fölkersahm, who returned from his Berlin sabbatical in 1845, rejoined the landtag. He resumed leading the agroliberal faction when announcing his voters would only oppose another expensive land survey from scratch if the landtag agreed to his original agrarian program. Fölkersahm also suggested replacing corvee with hard currency for tax payments and establishing independent, peasant credit unions to offer mortgages for private land ownership.

The nobility rejected this peasant credit union idea as too advantageous for the peasants. Others disputed the need to even

---

33. Bribery and corruption.

establish a peasant credit union, painting it as a needless competitor to the Livonian Nobility's Credit Union. When Fölkersahm questioned why this noble credit union had not yet sold more land to Latvian peasantry, the nobility countered: "Only with high interest rates can you tempt a baron into selling his land" (Švābe, 1958). Others feigned concern that Fölkersahm's peasant credit union would drive Latvians into enormous debt.[34]

Finally, in 1849, a decade after Fölkersahm entered the scene of allyship with Latvian peasants, the landtag of Livonia adopted a small reform that still mangled many of Fölkersahm's original tenets. As part of the 1849 resolution, peasants could now privately purchase a parcel of land (1/12 of a "ploughshare"– far too small to sustain a family) for six daalders. This concession was intentional; the nobility hoped to employ these pauperized Latvians at least part-time on the estates for still insignificant wages. The Act of 1849 also regulated the "country proletariat"- the landless, migratory farmhands who assisted a head of household in exchange for room and board. Hated by the nobility as "social parasites" because they remained outside of direct noble influence, these proletariat were frequently intimidated, obliged, or threatened by the police into taking permanent residency.

Fölkersahm died in 1856. Despite his charisma, lofty ideals, and persuasiveness, Fölkersahm's project of private peasant land ownership remained largely theoretical after his death. Although the landtag had finally accepted his proposals, from 1849-1864, Latvian peasants purchased only 209 farmsteads (0.5% of all farmsteads) in Livonia province, albeit still more than the mere 36 farmsteads purchased from 1823-1850. Four decades after serfdom's repeal

---

34. Debt that the Baltic German nobility didn't own.

in the Baltic, in 1858, 82% of peasants still satisfied their rental obligations with unpaid labor rather than cash (Švābe, 1958, pg. 147). Many attempts at peaceful protest had failed.

Despite the concessions Fölkersahm had yielded to the Baltic Germans in his projects, he remained an idealist and foresaw the turmoil awaiting Russia (the Revolution of 1905 and the Communist coup in 1917). Fölkersahm knew that the national welfare rested upon a strong tradition of independent, private landownership. In 1841, Fölkersahm wrote to a friend: "Private property was and remains the only natural cornerstone for a successful and prosperous peasantry" (Švābe, 1958, pg. 233). At the very minimum, his projects did function to solidify the distinction between individualist farmsteads of the Baltic ("viensētas) and the communal land tenure of Russia (sādžas) which analysts have used to justify a Russian communalist mindset versus a Latvian's individualism in the 20th century.

The First National Awakening

To prevent local labor shortages after untethering peasants from their estates in the early 19th century, clauses in Estonia and Courland were cooked up to prevent peasants from settling in cities until the provincial population had surpassed a benchmark. Only once the population grew past the benchmark, that surplus growth (above 120,000 people for example) would be allowed to resettle in provincial centers such as Riga, Jelgava, and Tallinn. Thus, in the Jelgava jail in 1838, 47% of the prisoners were held for not having valid passports to depart the countryside legally (Švābe, 1958, pg. 130). Oddly incongruous with the so-called sanctity of "free market principles", Latvians arrested here had merely left their estates according to the natural law of competition that Spanish-speaking "illegal" immigrants in the United States follow— for better wages from even the lowest, most undesirable urban jobs.

As newly urbanized Latvians increased their contacts with cultured Germans in the towns, negative perceptions of Latvians in cities congealed. Initial cultural differences with Baltic Germans reinforced many stereotypes about Latvians for decades hereafter. To escape these stereotypes, some Latvians adopted the German language to climb in socioeconomic standing; where social class and ethnicity were as inextricably linked as they were in the Baltic, many peasants shed (or tried to shed) their Latvian identities in exchange for more prestigious, German ones.

Like the many rural Mexicans in the 1970s and 80s forgoing their indigenous tongues for Spanish as new urbanites, many Latvians adopted German in the early 19th century for better careers in the towns and cities. Nonetheless, during the 19th century, the Latvian nation neither fully Germanized nor Russified enough to lose its national character. At that time, nothing intellectual was published in Latvian; as such, the first young, educated Latvians struggled to express themselves academically in their own mother language.

Until the mid-19th century, the Latvians truly were a people without a past or a future. It is illustrative that until Latvian linguists invented them in the 1870s, the language lacked not just words for 'past' or 'future' but also for concepts like: 'stairs,' 'fortress,' 'poem,' 'painting,' 'citizen,' 'subject,' 'constitution,' 'hospital,' 'hero,' 'letter,' 'history,' or 'science.' The mindset of the time stated that "an educated Latvian does not exist; an educated Latvian must necessarily become a German" (Švābe, 1958, pg. 370).

However, by writing and publishing Lāčplēsis between 1872 and 1887, Andrejs Pumpurs culminated the Latvian First National Awakening. Across Europe in the 19th century, people swapped their class identities for ones based upon language and ethnic traditions- their national ones. Concurrently, a group known today as the "New Latvians" (Jaunlatvieši) became the first educated generation of Latvians to reject Baltic German supremacy. In tandem with Russia's industrialization and serfdom's repeal across the empire in 1861, from the 1850-1870s the New Latvians redefined the Latvian identity. They asserted peasant demands and glorified peasant culture. Rejecting 'German' ways of thinking and being, they fleshed out newer 'Latvian' solutions to the Baltic's social inequities. Of course, Latvian nationalists and linguists worked to purge all German influence from the Latvian language, which was no easy feat either.

Despite its magnificent and imposing name, the 'First National Awakening' was hardly an all-encompassing movement, and certainly nothing that the contemporary Latvians knew they were participating in. It began in the 1850s at the extremely conservative University of Dorpat in modern Tartu, Estonia. Here, a small group of students gathered once a week to discuss how they might incorporate their 'mother tongue,' previously relegated to barnyards, into academia. The leader of these student meetings, a Latvian named Krišjānis Valdemārs, turned heads when he fixed the placard: "Kr. Valdemar – a Latvian" to his office door.

At that time, the saying: "born a Latvian, through education a German" characterized social boundaries across the Baltic. As students taught to think in German, the New Latvians of course struggled to formulate academic thoughts into their own first language. Until the National Awakening, most Baltic Germans dismissed the Latvian language as unnecessary for anything beyond steering a plow. During their time as students then, the New Latvians composed original poems, plays, and periodicals in the Latvian language to challenge this notion.

Whenever the Latvian language lacked terms to describe a concept or idea, the purists amongst them developed new words rather than borrowing from German or Russian. Juris Alunāns and Atis Kronvalds, New Latvians in the unique position of growing up in German-speaking families, were to Latvian wordsmithing what James Dean was to cinema – boundless creative forces immortalized by their early deaths. In his 37 years, Kronvalds coined roughly 200 words essential to modern Latvian today, including the terms for "the past" (pagātne), "the future" (nākotne), and "history" (vēsture). Alunāns, meanwhile, coined some 600 neologisms, most significantly replacing the German borrowings "kuchen" and "famīlija" with "virtuve" and "ģimene."

From academia, the New Latvians matured into activists. They published the dissident newspapers Mājas Viesis and Pēterburgas Avīzes to foster the everyday Latvian's knowledge of world events. They also polemicized with the Baltic German-subsidized newspaper Latweeschu Awises, a Latvian-language rag which upheld the traditional, conservative values. Denied from professional jobs in the Baltic like most other educated Latvians, Kr. Valdemārs founded Pēterburgas Avīzes after he moved to Petrograd, the imperial capital. Here, he reconnected with his former schoolmates from Dorpat and invited them to write for his newly established newspaper.

As chief editor of Pēterburgas Avīzes, Valdemārs was free to lampoon Baltic German supremacy from the safety of the imperial capital, while featuring popular science and practical knowledge articles in the Latvian language. In both Pēterburgas Avīzes and afterward, Valdemārs always stressed that the pathway to Latvian excellence lay foremost in private property ownership and maritime trade.

In 1861, the liberally minded Tsar Alexander II abolished serfdom across the Russian Empire. With this decree, all peasants were to receive plots of private land for themselves on credit, along with a transition from corvee to currency during the interim mortgage payments. However, as they often did, conservative Baltic Germans suppressed this news until it only reached Latvian readership via Pēterburgas Avīzes. Disgruntled, Latvian readers responded with protest petitions against the obscurantism of the Baltic Germans. In response, the Baltic Germans launched its own volley of viper strikes against the New Latvians for initiating the petitions and undermining traditional social mores.

In 1861, Professor Carl Christian Schirren disparaged the New Latvians: "There has never been, nor ever will be, nations in the Baltic- only conquerors and the conquered. The history of the land is stamped this way- as a colony... These five or six (New) Latvians, among whom only a few have even graduated university, use their education just to eat and drink at the same bar table with other peasants" (Švābe, 1958, pg. 368).

Another Baltic German, the Lutheran Pastor Gustav Brashe, wrote: "This little nation's fate is to be the same as all the others- the Livonians, Ingrians, Estonians- passing away while stillborn in the mother's womb. A Latvian has no semblance of a national past, recognizing himself only as a member of the peasantry. After the conquest,[35] he inherited only a crippled language and a hatred for Baltic Germans. In its time, this was a natural reaction, but today it is inexcusable- the Latvian has the German to thank for every improvement in life and his superior status to the Russian peasant [sic]" (Švābe, 1958, pg. 369).

While technically not incorrect that Latvians lacked a cohesive national past, the Baltic Germans disparaged them for it. As such, it fell to the Lāčplēsis myth for the Latvians to create a unifying national past, regardless of its historical accuracy.

Once again, as Pēterburgas Avīzes sold out from newsstands, the most conservative Baltic Germans invoked their "law and order" argument to stifle the newspaper's challenges. The general governor of Riga warned that the New Latvians only wanted political demonstration to topple the entire agrarian order of the Baltic[36]. Slander from the wealthy Baltic Germans prevailed, and after

---

35. The Northern Crusades (1201-1290).
36. This is exactly what they wanted.

multiple trips to a censor outside Valdemārs' hands, Pēterburgas Avīzes ceased publication in 1865. Meanwhile, after the peasant petitions, Riga's general governor ordered every peasant who had submitted a petition to be both investigated and prosecuted.

In 1865, the Baltic German nobility avenged their humiliation by sabotaging and incriminating Valdemārs with "defrauding" Latvian peasants. In 1863, Valdemārs had purchased land in the Novgorod governorate of Russia, far inland from the seaside or Petrograd, which he envisioned as a summer retreat for future affluent Latvians. In the newspaper, Valdemārs advertised parcels there for 15 rubles a unit, one-third to one-fifth the price that Baltic Germans were asking in the Baltic provinces. By the summer of 1864, through interpersonal connections and his skills in mass media, Valdemārs had sold every parcel of this "Letonija" colony.

Aware of this endeavor, agents of the Baltic nobility misinformed Courland's fishermen that the land at "Letonija" would be awarded to anyone for free, along with a "colonization stipend. They also promised the fishermen that parcels would face the seaside for income. As such, thousands of Latvian fishermen sold their belongings for almost nothing and stampeded to Novgorod in excitement. The fishermen arrived via railroad to discover Letonija hundreds of kilometers from the sea, a boggy taiga providing no opportunity whatsoever for catching fish.

After this, the federal government became involved in the "Letonija" scandal. As Baltic Germans were disproportionately over-represented within the imperial courts at Petrograd, they filed fraud charges against Valdemārs, arguing that he'd deceived peasants with his swampy, useless land. Legal debts bankrupted Valdemārs, estranging him from his brother in the process. Humiliated and penniless, Valdemārs fled to Moscow, where only after two decades did the police discontinue their surveillance of Valdemārs.

Delighted with their first entree, the Baltic Germans did not stop with Valdemārs to keep persecuting the New Latvians. They harassed the remaining journalists from Pēterburgas Avīzes, linking some to writings that ridiculed the Baltic Lutheran clergy, while implicating others in disseminating proclamations that called for the peasants to pillage and burn noble property. The authors of these "threatening letters" (signed simply "the incineration committee") were blacklisted forever from professional positions.

After the persecutions, nearly half of the New Latvian intellectuals joined Valdemārs in exile to Moscow. For example, after helping Latvian peasants to write petitions against Baltic Germans in 1863, Kaspars Biezbārdis was implicated in 'stoking unrest' and exiled. The author of many Darwinist translations and the compiler of thousands of Latvian folk songs, meanwhile, Kr. Barons, became a persona non-grata at all Baltic professions due to his "radical" liberal connections.

Matīss Kaudzītis, the author of the first work of Latvian literature, Mērnieku Laiki, summarized the New Latvians' reputation: "If someone was so inclined to take revenge against another, then all they needed then was to denounce that person as a 'New Latvian'. With this title alone, a victim was as good as ruined in Baltic society. Teachers and authors understood this; a denunciation could ruin someone just caught holding an edition of Pēterburgas Avīzes" (Švābe, 1958, pg. 366).

Andrejs Pumpurs, the author of Lāčplēsis, also described the New Latvians' fate: "Their individual destinies were nearly identical;

without any rights or prestige matching their qualifications, without belongings or provisions, sometimes even without a place to stay… they had to wander. [In Latvia] all doors were closed to them… With heavy hearts, they left their fatherland and travelled abroad, searching for room and board by teaching school lessons in Russia" (Švābe, 1958, pg. 366).

Kr. Valdemārs, leader of the New Latvian movement, even wrote in 1867: "In the Baltic Provinces, they will denounce anyone as a revolutionary, enemy of the state, barbarian, or fanatic, who sees the 1861 emancipation as a wise and just law" (Švābe, 1958, pg. 393).

Thus, many New Latvians and intellectuals followed those first Latvian Orthodox converts for a better life beyond Baltic German supremacy. Over the rest of the 19th century and until World War One, like the millions of black Americans fleeing the Jim Crow South in the Great Migration, a Latvian migration would siphon away five-sixths of Latvia's natural demographic growth.

The New Current (Jaunstrāvnieki) and 1905

On the eve of serfdom's repeal across the Russian Empire in 1861, the Baltic German nobility still profited foremost from distilling vodka. Throughout Livonia Province in 1860, there were five hundred distilleries producing seven million liters of vodka annually (Švābe, 1958, pg. 263). These distilleries supplied spirits to imperial banquets and peasant taverns alike, enabling alcoholism, domestic abuse, and liver cirrhosis for generations of Latvians. The reliance on vodka production for income also ensured the Baltic nobles would resist transitioning from corvee to wages for as long as possible.

After serfdom's empire-wide repeal in 1861, the Livonian nobility stalled in transitioning from corvee to currency until 1868, claiming a "lack of cash" prevented them from paying waged laborers. This intransigence even emboldened the Russian Empire's other aristocrats, such as those in the "black soil" regions of Ukraine, to adopt laws similar to the 1819 "land is mine, time is yours" model. With corvee's transition to cash successfully delayed by seven years, the Baltic Germans of Livonia only began selling peasants their land in 1868. Just four years later however, Livonia's peasantry had nonetheless mortgaged 25% of the province's area. Land privatization continued until around 1880, when it plateaued with 40% of the land under Latvian or Estonian peasant ownership.

Nonetheless, purchasing a private farmstead remained a gamble fit for only the most materially stable and risk tolerant Latvians. Sometimes land privatization was even more hazardous than just renting! Mortgages existed in thirty, fifty, or century term loans,[37] and

---

37. Had World War I not shattered Baltic German supremacy in Latvia, Latvians would have still been paying their mortgages until 1960 (Švābe, 1958, pg. 324).

Baltic Germans sold their land for prices three times higher than in Pskov, Petrograd, or even the fantastically fertile Black-Soil Ukraine.[38]

Reincarnating the early 19th century's "free contract," Baltic Germans also encumbered their sales with clauses obliging the buyer to benefit them personally.[39] Some denied the buyer their rights to harvest timber or hunt and fish the property, as these activities were traditionally reserved for the nobility. Many contracts guaranteed the seller's right to inspect the buyer's farmstead at any time during repayment; if "evidence" arose indicating neglect or laxity, the seller could petition a court to declare the buyer incompetent for the rest of his mortgage.[40] Finally, sales included clauses stating that a single missed payment could legally cancel the sale without recompense.[41] In this way, conservative Baltic Germans bankrupted the life savings of some Latvian peasants during the 1870s and 1880s.

Latvian peasants, as private landowners finally, now technically qualified for admittance into the governing Livonian landtag. Be it so, the conservative Baltic Germans refused to part with any of their historical ethnic or class privilege by accepting Latvians into the local government. From 1864-1882, the Riga landtag issued annual denials to many land-owning Latvians who had petitioned for admission to the provincial congress.

---

38. Latvian peasants could purchase land in the Petrograd or Pskov governorates for 22 to 27 rubles; the same area in Livonia sold for 68 rubles (Švābe, 1958, pg. 320).

39. Such as maintaining estate roads or bridges as in corvee.

40. By court order, the seller could then demand his entire remaining sale balance within three months or reappropriate the entire property, including monies already paid.

41. From 1886-1896, credit unions holding peasant mortgages auctioned off 3926 farmsteads, half of which had nearly paid off their mortgages (Švābe, 1958, pg. 529).

Because of absurdly high land prices in the Baltic, thousands of other Latvians left their homeland to settle the wilderness due east. In 1859, the New Latvian Juris Alunāns encouraged Latvians to emigrate to Russia by writing: "If one cannot make ends meet in his fatherland, then it's better to leave for where one fares better" (Švābe, 1958, pg. 379). As a result, from 1882-1899, 83% of Livonia's natural population growth heeded Alunāns' call and migrated away from Latvia. In 1904, when 15% (250,000) of all Latvians already lived outside the homeland, the Trans-Siberian railway had opened the Russian Pacific to yet more Latvian colonists (Švābe, 1958, pg. 724). For this reason, Latvia and Estonia remained chronically underpopulated amidst the decades of Russification in the late 1800s.

Thanks to inflated land prices, vast sums of silver rubles (77.3 million) meanwhile flowed into noble coffers after the land sales (Švābe, 1958, pg. 318). The Baltic Germans invested this capital in factories and warehouses rather than raising wages to attract laborers back to the estates. By buying factories in the burgeoning cities, the barons chased a new, urban labor force only recently free from the countryside themselves. Working under abominable conditions in the factories, by 1905, many of these workers had encountered Marxist ideologies before congealing into communist cells.

As the New Latvian movement fractioned Latvians generationally between pro-German and New Latvian camps, land privatization stratified them socioeconomically and ideologically. Thus, this era was characterized by a sharp ideological divide between "the Latvian farmer and his farmhand." Janis Jansons-Brauns, a Latvian Social Democrat and member of the "New Current" generation, wrote: "Marxism made us aware that the Latvian nation was divided into classes, each with its own interests, opinions, and efforts, and that the Latvian proletariat was the class which would build the future." (Švābe, 1958, pg. 648). This "New Current" (Jaunstrāvnieki) came of age amidst the land privatization and Russification. As students and young adults, they felt disillusioned by the lack of social progress preceding them that Latvian nationalism had once promised. They perceived a 'hollowness' to the patriotism of the New Latvians, which yielded almost no tangible improvements to their everyday lives. And whereas the first National Latvian Song and Dance Festivals (1873, 1880, 1888) enchanted the older generation of middle-aged New Latvians, the "New Current" generation derided these as 'the intelligentsia's festival.'[42] Deeper ideas from Europe enthralled the New Current- the messianic promises of Marx and Engels, a restructuring of society, and communism's foretelling of a Global Revolution.

The 1880's also brought state-sponsored Russification to the previously autonomous Baltic.[43] By law, courts and schools switched exclusively to the Russian language for instruction, while office and store signage appeared only in Cyrillic, and whole towns and cities were sometimes renamed.[44] For Latvian teenagers, Russian became the sole language permissible to use at school. This generation, learning to read and think exclusively in Russian, infused their speech with Russian jargon like the previous generation's use of German.

---

42. "Song festivals are not the nation's, but the intelligentsia's festival. The wealthiest arrange these celebrations to distract from their capitalist designs. Organizers feign innocence by wearing "national" rags and entertaining us at this freakshow" (Švābe, 1958, pg. 516).
43. In the 1897 census, the Russian Empire had 125.6 million inhabit- ants, with Russians composing just 44.3% of the populace. Baltic Germans disproportion- ately dominated the government and military. Russification intended, thus, to unify the empire according to one language and to reduce internal discord.
44. On school maps, Dinaburg became Dvinsk (Двинск), Dorpat became Jurjev (Юрьев), and the Daugava River became the Zapadnaya Dvina (Западная Двина). Catholic Latvians were also henceforth classified as "Belarussians."

In the style of the New Latvians a generation before, students of the New Current gathered in the evenings to socialize, discuss ideas, and practice rhetoric. These gatherings dove into questions deeper than of their predecessors, however: of migrant labor, feminism, and the 'banality' of Latvian patriotism without material improvements. When Riga's German-language newspapers accidentally exposed these youth to Marxist excerpts by publishing a portion of the Communist Manifesto to ridicule it, the New Current gladly adopted Marx for their discussion. Like any other youthful group eager to overthrow the existing order of their parents, the New Current aspired to shatter the old traditions, awaken society, and rejuvenate the human race through any means possible.

Instead of having one leader like Kr. Valdemārs was to the New Latvians, the New Current had two: Jānis Rainis – Latvia's national poet, and Pēteris Stučka – a future Bolshevik and member of Lenin's inner circle. The two were classmates in high school and studied law together in Petrograd. They diverged as the New Current crystalized its philosophy in adulthood; Rainis, who reincarnated Lāčplēsis through his 1905 play "Fire and Night" (Uguns un Nakts), believed national culture and socialism could be interwoven. Stučka regarded the 'nation' as superfluous, framing his worldview entirely through a lens of the working class's struggle against the bourgeoisie.

According to Kārlis Kasparsons, another New Current Latvian, with the group's first exposure to Marxism in 1890, the New Current almost unanimously rejected its 'internationalist' component. Nonetheless, as the New Current developed its ideals in the newspaper Dienas Lapa, their views steadily drifted left. Long before writing Uguns un Nakts and becoming Latvia's national poet, in the 1890s, Rainis edited one of Riga's most radical, socialist periodicals. He wrote in his memoirs: "In 1893, I brought a suitcase packed with socialist literature home from Germany. From this bag, I planted the seed for the entire socialist movement in Latvia" (Švābe, 1958, pg. 522).

Like the New Latvians before them, members of the New Current matured from academia to activism. They organized "educational" evenings for dockyard workers in Riga and other port cities, 'evangelizing' them with Marxist theory like the Moravians almost two centuries earlier. The western port of Liepāja had the most religious sects of any city in the Baltic, and Marxism found success here "only because the inhabitants were so prepared to accept any pathway to salvation" (Švābe, 1958, pg. 524). Meanwhile, thanks to the 1730's Moravian missionaries, by the time of the New Current, Latvians were one of the most literate ethnicities in the Russian Empire. This skill predisposed them to encountering written Marxist tenants first.

In 1895, using their newly-adopted Marxist ideologies, the Latvian Social Democrats began organizing labor strikes against the Baltic German factory owners. Labor strikes in Petrograd's textile factories in 1896 secured an 11.5-hour workday, further emboldening the Latvian Social Democrats. From 1899-1903, labor strikes rocked the Russian Empire on almost a daily basis, many of them in the Baltic. With education and training from the Latvian Social Democrats, in May 1899, the women of Riga's textile factories in Džūte went on strike for higher wages.

The years of labor strikes culminated when the Russian Empire entered war with Japan in 1904. This mismanaged and deeply unpopular conflict sparked an empire-wide revolt in 1905, which Lenin later described as his "Great Dress Rehearsal" for his Bolshevik Coup in 1917. Already with the start of hostilities against Japan, a

Social Democrat committee in Liepāja invited workers to withdraw their savings from banks and create a currency shortage for the government. Next, hundreds of imperial soldiers in Latvia refused to even climb aboard their warships to Japan. Regardless of boarding these ships later at gunpoint, the soldiers still mutinied afterward while in route to the Far East. Meanwhile, back in the Baltic, young Latvians marched to revolutionary hymns during their training exercises and waved red bandanas from their windows.

With this anti-war sentiment and a youthful population, labor strikes that began in Petrograd quickly spread to the rest of the Empire. Although the Baltic theater of the 1905 revolution unfolded first amongst factory workers in Riga, it climaxed in the countryside, pitting landless peasants and Social Democrats against the Baltic German nobility. Thus, the "class struggle" in Latvia necessarily unfolded as an ethnic one.

In March of 1905, estate servants outside Liepāja went on strike for higher wages and shorter workdays, while on the outskirts of Riga, landless peasants boycotted their rent payments and auctions of other, evicted peasants' belongings. Heedless to these concerns, the German barons enlisted the police to punish the disobedience, driving servants from their apartments. The disaffected Latvians physically left their employers by torching estate forests and warehouses as they walked away.

Proclaiming party slogans from Riga meanwhile, the Social Democrats called on the landed nobility to sell their land for competitive and realistic prices, insisting that "no one with his own corner of land ("savs stūrītis zemes") joins a rebellion" (Švābe, 1958, pg. 594). The Social Democrats demanded that the nobility pay its fair share of taxes and provide free schooling in the Latvian language. Nonetheless, the conservative Baltic Germans ignored these warnings, just as they ignored Garlieb Merkel a century earlier. On 17 estates in June, the Social Democrats organized strikes during critical times for the planting to force these issues. One strike with 30,000 farmworkers outside Jelgava even secured a 300-ruble annual minimum wage (Švābe, 1958, pg. 597).

To enforce solidarity with a strike, some Social Democrats walked from farmstead to farmstead and forced peasants to stop working. They convinced disaffected laborers to march to the estates and disarm the police. Sometimes, the Social Democrats even persuaded their strikers to kindle fires under the tsar's portrait, conscription lists, and other records at county courthouses. In thirty counties, Latvian strikers demolished walls, distilleries, and taverns; others cut down telegraph poles and dislodged railroad tracks.

During the revolution, Social Democrats practiced disrupting Lutheran services of unpopular ministers across Latvia.[45] During the liturgy, usually after the pastor mentioned the noble patron's name, professional agitators heckled the pastor in his pulpit. From the altars, they then led revolutionary songs, and, at a few churches, forced the minister to carry the red revolutionary flag on a march. Five Lutheran pastors were assassinated during 1905, and a few dozen churches shuttered. This agitation was confined exclusively to Lutheran churches, never appearing in Catholic churches nor Orthodox ones (Švābe, 1958, pg. 655).

---

45. At the turn of the 20th century, the Lutheran Church was still the mouthpiece for Baltic German supremacy it had been since the 1700s; 80% of pastors in Livonia and 70% in Courland were ethnic Germans (Švābe, 1958, pg. 654). The noble landowners still hand-picked the clergymen, who in turn reinforced traditional class and ethnic roles. To combat labor shortage from mass emigration, Lutheran ministers preached that leaving rural life for the city was against the natural order— it was God's will that a Latvian remain a ploughman (Švābe, 1958, pg. 333).

With mayhem and supply chain disruptions occurring in Riga, the Russian Empire's third largest port by that time, the Russian government declared martial law in the Baltic in August. From exile in London, Lenin immediately called for a "dictatorship of the proletariat," while the Mensheviks[46] and more moderate Latvian Social Democrats encouraged unity and dialogue with other parties for a Russian parliament. On August 23, the imperial government signed a truce with Japan- a loss particularly humiliating for any racist Western power. Hopes that this truce would placate society proved unfounded; in October, striking railroad workers halted imperial train traffic. Telegraph and telephone service were then discontinued, and when Petrograd's water supply failed, the imperial court urged the tsar to release his October Manifesto. In this document, twelve years before his deposal in 1917, Tsar Nikolai II agreed to a limited monarchy, representative government, and a constitution.

In areas of Latvia with interrupted state authority, the Social Democrats organized "soviets" (worker councils) at the parish level. This "socialism from below" allowed government resolutions to come directly from Latvian mouths. At their November congress, Social Democrats announced the rural Latvians' demands- to abolish the police[47], repeal the patron's right of choosing religious leaders, close distilleries, and initiate a progressive income tax for the populace.[48]

Despite the October Manifesto's concessions, in November 1905, a mass paranoia swept the Baltic with the year's fading

---

46. The less radical wing of the Social-Democrat movement, opposed to Bolshevik extremism and for social justice.
47. Like the Latvian calls to "abolish the police" in 1905 for their abuse of authority, black Americans today have as much legitimacy in demanding the same.
48. In 1905, Baltic Germans owned 46.4% of the land in Livonia but paid only 8.3% of the province's tax burden (Švābe, 1958, pg. 652). Despite having made 80 million rubles from peasant land sales by 1900, they contributed nothing to peasant welfare, granaries, or schoolhouse upkeep.

daylight. Urban and rural Latvians alike shuddered overhearing rumors that the "Black Hundreds," a Russian paramilitary group, had arrived to restore order to the still restive Baltic. Undercover as these apocryphal "boogey-men," Baltic German police attacked a schoolhouse containing a Latvian workers' council, whom they imprisoned and tortured in a castle dungeon. When Latvian militia arrived and discovered their countrymen groaning and half-alive, they threatened to kill their own Baltic German prisoners. Thus, to halt yet more bloodshed, the Baltic Germans agreed to repeal martial law in the Baltic, although they later reneged after the prisoner swap and shot 90 Latvian peasants anyway (Švābe, 1958, pg. 622).

During November and December of 1905, 288 arsons broke out in Livonia province and 148 in Courland (Švābe, 1958, pg. 627). In Latvian cultural memory, the image of a "burning manor" still embodies the year 1905, although arson did not represent the average striker's mentality. The petroleum needed to ignite a brick building demanded more resources than average peasants could provide, which suggests that urban Bolsheviks (Stučka's men) were the more likely culprits.[49] Like the white nationalists and young, male adventurists swooping into Minneapolis from as far as Texas after George Floyd's murder in 2020 (Self-Described Member of "Boogaloo Bois" Charged with Riot, 2020), the Latvian national struggle became muddled with another, more malignant one.

Infuriated by the uptick in arson despite his concessions to create a parliament, the tsar ordered his soldiers to "arrest less and shoot more" by the end of December. Dividing the Baltic into nine districts, Nikolai II permitted the military to suppress revolt

---

49. This theory is supported by the fact many arsons centered outside large cities (Riga and Liepaja), which were Bolshevik control-centers (Švābe, 1958, pg. 627).

by any means necessary. Court martials occurred at noble estates; punishments were delivered as they once had been in the 1700's; women, children, and the elderly were driven through rows of 300 soldiers swinging chains, rods, and leather belts.

After suppressing 1905's unrest, punitive expeditions continued until the fall of 1908. Surprise assassinations sometimes occurred when transferring Latvian prisoners by road to another prison- these prisoners were classified as "attempting escape" and any further investigation promptly concluded. During the 1905 uprisings, 82 Baltic Germans were killed, while the punitive expeditions eliminated 2,600 Latvian peasants (Švābe, 1958, pg. 632). The death toll for Latvians after 1905 was even greater than in the 1919 Latvian War of Independence (1,748). Still further, 7,000 other Latvian "revolutionaries" served the rest of their lives in forced labor camps,[50] and 5,000 more escaped to the Americas – Brazil, Argentina, Canada, and the United States.

Insurgents evading capture after 1905 fought on for several years as "Forest Brothers."[51] Living in groups of 10-15 men, they survived under the illusion that the revolution would never be defeated. These young men continued their partisan attacks, with sympathetic Latvian peasants initially supporting them with groceries, clothing, and intelligence. As the imperial army's presence further burdened Latvian peasants however, sympathy for the Forest Brothers waned. Demoralized elements amongst the Forest Brothers attacked not only soldiers but also wealthier peasants for provisions. Garrisons

50. Although Latvians composed 1.5% of the Russian Empire's population, they comprised 10-12% of all Siberian deportees (Švābe, 1958, pg. 632). In America, 38% of the prison population is black though black Americans account for just 13% nationally.
51. The term "Forest Brother" is a recurring term to describe guerilla warfare throughout Latvian history. Following World War II, "Forest Brothers" led a ten-year resistance into the 1950's against the Soviet Occupation.

of imperial soldiers, meanwhile, conscripted non-partisan Latvians as night watchmen or employing them by day to comb the forests for fugitives. Without the peasant support, by the winter of 1906- 1907, the last Forest Brothers laid down their arms.

In March of 1906, after appraising the arson done to Baltic German properties, Nikolai II approved a 1.6-million-ruble loan to compensate for their incinerated splendors (Švābe, 1958, pg. 629). While historians may lament those artworks, libraries, and archives lost in 1905, they also acknowledge that the treasures symbolized the Baltic's unjust agrarian order at that time. For instance, during the revolution's aftermath, the phrase: "For every German, twelve Latvians!" circulated amongst Germans. Hearing this, the punitive expeditions torched 70 Latvian peasant houses, detonated one school, and ruined the life savings of 300 Latvian private landowners as retribution[52] (Švābe, 1958, pg. 629).

After 1905, the newspaper and press coverage characterized the mentalities of Baltic society in the early 20th century. The conservative German-language press insisted that "only the Latvian's poor overall character and ungratefulness" had fueled rebellion, and that the Baltic was a fair society otherwise. Other Baltic German publications faulted the nobles themselves for not Germanizing the peasantry sooner when it was "still possible."[53] The Lutheran clergy contended that the revolution had no socioeconomic causes whatsoever, and it was only stoked by "those unsuccessful in life, the renters wanting to become overnight property owners" (Švābe, 1958, pg. 645).

---

52. Private landowners saddled with mortgages were the most risk averse and participated the least in 1905. Nonetheless, these apolitical Latvians incurred material losses of 2 million rubles during the punitive expeditions (Švābe, 1958, pg. 629).
53. Before the New Latvians emerged.

From their illicit printing presses meanwhile, the Social Democrats continued propagandizing Marxism, publishing wild and fabricated victory accounts to maintain the fighting spirit. "All the Russian proletariat gazes with amazement at the tiny Baltic, where the multi-national proletariat fights shoulder-to-shoulder... Comrades! In the name of Latvian Social Democrats, we salute your victories!" (Švābe, 1958, pg. 624)

Latvia's national poet and former Social Democrat, Jānis Rainis, wrote of the 1905 Revolution afterward: "Serious German publishers and even a few Russians say that the Latvians want to separate from Russia... but I can categorically say that no one intends this. Never once in 1905 did the insurgents cite a 'Latvian republic' as their mission, although the Baltic Germans called those democratically elected councils "republics" to frighten the Russian bureaucracy. The Revolution of 1905 wasn't a chimeric, nationalist revolt, but an uprising of the lower classes demanding that the barons renounce their privilege and accept a democratic government" (Švābe, 1958, pg. 647).

Indeed, the lack of Latvian political or cultural initiative during 1905 was a remarkable outlier; while the Lithuanians to the south demanded a restored, autonomous state, and Estonians to the north demanded political separation from Latvian-speaking areas of Livonia province, hardly any Latvians mentioned 'cultural autonomy' let alone political independence (Švābe, 1958, pg. 615).

Nonetheless, because of the Revolution's destruction to private property as in 2020's Minneapolis, the imperial government finally conceded to a limited monarchy and representative democracy through parliament. Censorship of the press loosened for a time in Russia, and restrictions on public expression and gatherings relaxed.

Socialist advertisements even reappeared legally in the newspapers. Although the tsar dissolved first two parliaments ("Duma") for failing to discharge their duties in a manner agreeable to him, the Russian Empire's people still gained their first experience in representative democracy.

Furthermore, the 1905 uprising infused Latvians with a modest taste for self-determination. In World War I, memories of 1905 inspired Latvians to form the Latvian Riflemen's brigade in 1915. In those early years on the Eastern Front, the Riflemen fought some of Russia's most ferocious battles, accepting and succeeding at missions that others refused. As the war dragged on however, the jaded and burned-out Riflemen shifted their allegiance to Bolshevism.

Ironically, and totally contradicting my vehement anti-communist childhood, by helping to consolidate Soviet power in Russia, only the Latvian Riflemen legitimized Latvian statehood in Western eyes. After World War I, the capitalist West relied on the Latvian republic for a "sanitary line" against such an unacceptable neighbor as the Soviet Union. In the event of a monarchist victory in the Russian Civil War, the Western powers were prepared only to accept a return to Russia's pre-war imperial borders, including all of Baltic. However, the Latvian Riflemen secured so many decisive victories for the Soviet Union, that the monarchist Russians never returned to power. Latvia's Red Riflemen thus propped up the Soviet Union, the only force whose existence made the West willing to accept Latvian, national statehood. (The Soviet Union, which Latvian Riflemen propped up, also illegally reoccupied Latvia in 1940.)

However, the Latvian Red Riflemen did not secure Latvian statehood alone, even if Latvia's nationalist forces were fewer in number than them. At times, the future president of Latvia, Kārlis

Ulmanis, embodied the entire Latvian government in his one person. Heeding Ulmanis' courage and determination, other Latvians grabbed weapons to fight for their statehood in 1919, many believing in the unifying (but apocryphal) national legend of Lāčplēsis when doing so. Later, the national poet, Jānis Rainis, even revised his views of the Latvian state. Where in 1905 he saw the Latvians as merely a social class of the proletariat, in 1911, he summarized his nation's destiny in the line of his play Indulis un Ārija: "We are a small tribe, but we will be as great as our will affords us" (Švābe, 1958, pg. 656).

Pirmais Pasaules Karš (World War I)

A wooden sign attached to a string in a Latvian museum today reads "Today, I spoke in Latvian" (Я сегодня говориль по латышски). This sign was used analogously to the "dunce hat," whereby the Latvian pupil would wear it around their neck to shame them for speaking Latvian. As such, by 1914, Russification was so complete in the Baltic provinces that one could not even purchase a train ticket without speaking Russian or using an interpreter.

If in the early 1800s, when 90% of Latvia's population could be considered ethnic Latvian, after decades of Russification and industrialization leading up to World War I, Latvians now made up only 60% of the population now (Švābe, 1958, pg. 724). As ethnic Latvians emigrated Siberia or Ukraine to escape Baltic German prejudice, simultaneous industrialization attracted hordes of non-Latvian immigrants from the rest of the Empire.

Before World War I, Latvians also had among the slowest natural growth rates of any ethnicity in the Russian empire; Latvian marriages produced 3.1 children per marriage while the average family in Russia produced 5.3 children (Švābe, 1958, pg. 700). Of the 50 governorates of European Russia, Courland and Livonia provinces had the very lowest birth rates in 1913. And if across European Russia during those pre-war years, the average rate was 43.9 births per 1000 people, then in Courland it was only 24.6 births, and in Livonia 22.6 (Švābe, 1958, pg. 699).

These non-competitive birthrates, combined with the yearly net emigration of Latvians, threatened the nation's very viability. As mentioned before, the specter of national extinction is omnipresent for Latvians; in 1915, when the German Empire occupied Courland, two thirds of the province's population had already fled as refugees, which encouraged German officers to consider colonizing western Latvia with German settlers.

As early as 1907, Baltic German barons in Courland (K. Manteuffel) began snapping up foreclosed properties to resettle with ethnic Germans. In 1905, K Manteifels witnessed firsthand the arson of his property in Kazdanga; afterward, he wanted to de-Latvianize Courland to prevent such an uprising from ever reoccurring. After acquiring some 47,000 hectares of land, his initiative invited German colonists living in Ukraine and along the Volga River to re-settle to these properties. Offering them 10 to 25-hectare plots for only 600-1500 rubles, the initiative attracted some 20,000 ethnic Germans to Latvia (Švābe, 1958, pg. 668).

Simultaneously, the tsarist government resumed the tempo of Russification after recovering from its paralysis in 1905. From 1909-1914, the federal government purchased private estates across the Baltic and prioritized selling them to ethnic Russians to alter the ethnic character of the Baltic. While the Latvian peasants and Baltic German nobles weren't explicitly excluded from purchasing these properties, the government incentivized ethnic Russians to colonize them by charging only 10% down-payments from Russians and subsidizing the purchase price (Švābe, 1958, pg. 669).

Nonetheless, while the Latvian nation languished, Riga's population before World War I ballooned into one of the empire's five largest cities. As a leading global timber port, Riga handled the greatest percentage of Russia's exports in 1913 at 28.2% (Švābe, 1958, pg. 687). Without World War I's interruption, Riga might have even grown to a million inhabitants, rivaling with Moscow, Petrograd, or Kyiv. And thanks to the Baltic's ice-free ports, even tiny Ventspils on the northwest coast competed with the ice-bound imperial capital, Petrograd, for Russia's international trade.

Despite the imperial parliament established after 1905, the empire's conservative inertia also prevented further meaningful reform from succeeding after 1905; in 1910, Latvian peasants still footed 90% of the tax burden while they controlled only 40% of the land (Švābe, 1958, pg. 694). Surveys of the factory workers in Riga after 1905 found them just as predisposed to alcoholism and as apathetic as before the revolution. Voter suppression before 1907's Third Parliamentary Elections secured 50.5% of the parliament's deputies for noble interests and only 22.5% for the peasantry's, rendering the Duma meaningless (Švābe, 1958, pg. 675). Ultimately, well-entrenched powers in the Russian Empire ensured that little would change despite 1905.

After 1905, the Latvian intelligentsia also went underground, living abroad in exile or melting into the anonymity of Russia's industrial cities. Jānis Rainis refined his political views while writing Latvian theater from Switzerland, but in Petrograd, Pēteris Stučka crystallized his idea that the next revolution needed to abolish even small private farm holdings for being too inefficient. Nonetheless, the moderate and radical Latvians continued attacking one another in the press, while the newspapers of Baltic German sympathizers applauded the overall harshness of 1906's punitive expeditions.

Like the Latvians in hell's boiling kettle dragging one another back down, the Latvians before World War I tore at each politically, through newspaper diatribes, or by informing on each other to tsarist police. Unlike the Russian and Jewish women who loved their husbands more deeply, the grave-tending Latvians instead approached minority-hood in their own homeland by 1914. "Politically divided and without national goals or international connections, the First World War exploded behind our backs" (Švābe, 1958, pg. 734).

In August 1914, Russia entered World War I by invading Germany through East Prussia. In the Battle of Augustów in modern Poland, Imperial regiments with 85% of their regiments being ethnic Latvian scored an important battle victory. Nonetheless, because of overextension and blunders by leadership, during this entire operation, 100,000 Imperial soldiers fell or were injured, and 100,000 more were captured (Andersons, 1967, pg. 38). The initial Russian invasion of the German Empire collapsed.

The author in 2014 outside the Kazdanga Manor, a former property of Manteuffel

"The Latvians shed their blood— the Russians gained the fame." 20,000 of Russia's first casualties were Latvian soldiers, alongside Lithuanians and Estonians. The Latvians thus went into the pages of history as the "heroic sons of Russia", while only the families of the fallen recognized their true losses. (Andersons, 1967, pg. 38).

As the empire's newspapers skimmed over Russia's military failures, in the fall of 1914, the government began persecuting its Baltic Germans to distract from the languishing war effort. Although many Germans were Russia's most competent civil servants, the paranoid tsarist government nonetheless fired them from their posts, conducted mass arrests, and searched their houses. The government later deported 33 Baltic German ministers to Siberia and outlawed publicly speaking German in Riga for a time.

As the anti-German hysteria spread that winter of 1914-1915, many Latvians denounced their Baltic German employers. After Latvian-language newspapers rewarded tips on suspicious persons or behaviors, many Latvians suddenly "discovered" airports, weapons, or secret fuel caches connected to noble estates. Upon closer investigation, most of these tips were debunked, and so the Latvians began turning on one another. Observing this behavior, and already suspicious of the Latvians since 1905, the Russian government ignored requests to establish an all-Latvian division within the army.

In spring of 1915, the German Empire invaded the Russian Baltic. When news reports arrived of oncoming German troops, Tsar Nikolai II ordered all Jews expelled from Lithuania as potential sympathizers and traitors. 30,000 were deported to Riga, some inside locked train cars, many starving to death in route (Andersons, 1967, pg. 63). Since Jews composed large portions of the military's medical staff, the tsar's paranoia only harmed his army and its chances for success.

To deprive the encroaching Germans of comfort or aid, the Russians next conducted a scorched-earth retreat from Courland on the magnitude of Moscow's arson ahead of Napoleon in 1812. At first, all men of working age living in Courland were ordered to evacuate the province and mobilize to the army. Next, the Russian cavalry confiscated the peasantry's horses, returning later for their other livestock to provide the army's rations. To starve the German army before their arrival, grain in the field was destroyed, which the government promised to repay to the peasant at an undefined date.[54]

In April of 1915, after burning nearly everything flammable in Courland, the Russian army whipped up an unprecedented panic amongst Courland's peasantry. Combined with another wave of migrants in July 1915 from Riga, at the Great War's very beginning, one third of Latvia' s inhabitants had fled their homes and left Latvia (Andersons, 1967, pg. 67). This far exceeding any numeric losses Latvia suffered during the Holocaust or in World War II. And whilst the Russians evicted Latvians from their homes and burned their properties behind them, German airplanes dropped proclamations inviting Latvians to greet the German army as liberators. Nonetheless, the Latvians still saw less risk in cooperating with their reckless, Russian government than in siding with compatriots of the hated Baltic Germans.

In 1915, 400,000 Latvian refugees left Courland with a million livestock, goats, and pigs (Andersons, 1967, pg. 65). In such close contact, foot-and-mouth disease spread amongst the cattle, while pig and goat carcasses littered the roadsides. Oncoming cavalrymen sometimes trampled small domestic animals, and whenever rumors circulated that the German army was approaching, the refugees stampeded too, leaving behind broken wheels and crying, lost children.

---

54. For their lost property, the refugees were given certificates to verify their belongings' destruction on government orders. Amidst the chaos of the war, most of these paper certificates were torn, soaked, or lost. To further complicate compensation, some certificates further required an eyewitness to verify the owners' identity, rendering many worthless.

From Riga, trains ferried these refugees further to Pskov, Vitebsk, and other cities of western Russia, while the remaining Latvians traveled by horse and cart. An eyewitness describes the scene: "Families covered in sweat, exhaustion, and coal dust travelled with only the belongings they could pile onto their overloaded carts. Fallen livestock littered the roadsides as Cossacks cut their way through the cattle with whips. Families lost contact with one another, sometimes for life. The people were fearful, desperate, and eventually – apathetic" (Andersons, 1967, pg. 66).

As the German army captured one town after another in Courland, the Russian military cobbled together a Latvian volunteer unit for the defense of Riga. When these Latvians unexpectedly halted a German advance on Riga, the Germans elected to pause their assault and sit along the Daugava River instead. After this unexpected heroism, and with memories of 1905 still fresh in their minds, some Latvians suggested establishing an ethnic Latvian rifleman's brigade. While the local Baltic Germans tried to derail this proposal, by mid-August, the first formations of the Latvian Riflemen were already recruiting volunteers.

As the German army camped just outside Riga in July 1915, the second exodus of Baltic citizens matched the first one from Courland in size. The Russians ordered Riga, largest of Russia's ports, to be evacuated along with its factory equipment, machinery, and labor force ahead of a German invasion. When the government ordered Riga's heavy industry to be transported to the interior, factories were instead looted, damaged, or scrapped in the frenzy. By August, when the German army had stabilized their positions along the Daugava just outside Riga, the city's population had dropped from 507,000 to 231,000. Furthermore, in 1915, the governorate of

Courland's population had fallen fell from 812,000 to just 245,000 (Andersons, 1967, pg. 67).

In September 1915, Tsar Nikolai II overtook command of the armed forces after his generals repeatedly failed on the battlefield. Nonetheless, through the mud and autumn rains of 1915 and despite Russia's incompetent leadership, the Latvian Riflemen defended Riga. The vast, sphagnum bogs west and south of Riga forced the armies to engage one another at choke points, favoring defenders. Amidst aerial bombardments of Riga's bridges and railways, and under the cover of rain and darkness, Latvian Riflemen sometimes waded up to their knees through bogs to flush the Germans from their positions.

If in April of 1915, the empire's newspapers regarded Latvia as just another "third rate field" ("trešās šķiras lauks"), then by autumn of 1915, the Russian government wanted the Latvian Riflemen to hold the Daugava front at any cost. This, of course, didn't account for the tsar's personal disdain for Latvians; when Tsar Nikolai II visited the Baltic front in mid-November, he completely ignored the Latvian Riflemen and shunned them from participating in a military parade. Influenced by the Empress, a German herself, the tsar scorned the Latvian boys despite them being his best soldiers.

During all of 1916, the tsar burned through his Latvian forces. Ordering attacks in March, Tsar Nikolai amassed 12 000 Latvian Riflemen. These soldiers sank to their knees in mud and cold water during the spring thaw, failing however to capture any territory. During another offensive in July of 1916, the Imperial artillery stirred up so much muck with its poorly aimed artillery fire that the Germans pinpointed their positions and destroyed them without suffering a single casualty.

Despite the Tsar's scorn for the Latvians, in late 1916, an Imperial general applauded the Latvian accomplishments of the preceding year. Despite the Latvians' insignificance until this time, their discipline and military success had immortalized their name across Russia; after all, they'd captured German positions the Russians viewed as "unobtainable." Therefore, the general hoped the Riflemen could repeat their successes on a much grander scale; the Germans would expect an attack the least during the Orthodox Christmas of January. And so began the fateful "Christmas Battles."

Leading up to the offensive, the Latvian Riflemen trained in nighttime warfare and stealth operations to penetrate the German defenses. They practiced cutting barbed wire fences like what the Germans had barricaded their main fortification with, west of Riga, at "Machine Gun Hill" (Ložmetējkalns). Nonetheless, the first night of the operation, in January 1917, was frigid. The bogs west of Riga were frozen solid, and a powerful blizzard impeded movement. Wearing white camouflage, the Latvian fence-cutters silently snipped passageways through the German razor labyrinth.

In some places, ten successive lines of barbed wire came with an occasional live electric current. Trenches followed the wire, followed by nine-foot walls soaked in water before they had frozen. Behind these walls, the Germans established machine gun "nests" to shelter in. Older and more mature than the Latvians, the seasoned Germans felt confident in their defenses.

During the Christmas Battles, many of the Latvian boys "believed in miracles" (Andersons, 1967, pg. 128). Indeed, it was a miracle at all that the Latvians captured a 4 km wide territory in the bog, forest, and traps west of Riga. Nonetheless, this new protrusion was indefensible, with snow drifts replacing bunkers where the frozen ground prevented the Latvians from digging-in. The Christmas Battles concluded after only a week of horrific Latvian casualties in what was later called the "Blizzard of Souls" (Dvēseļu Putenis).

With so much death and mismanagement during the Christmas Battles, the Riflemen remained at only a third of their original membership afterward. As a result, with Latvian troops all along the Daugava demoralized by 1917, Latvian Bolsheviks (the former Social Democrats) easily infiltrated their ranks. Though initially dismissed by the Rifleman, these Bolsheviks soon captivated the Riflemen with promises of Global Revolution and a messianic, classless society. If at the beginning of 1917, these disillusioned Riflemen began to insubordinate their commanders, then by October, they would facilitate the overthrow of the interim government in Petrograd. And after becoming the Latvian "Red Riflemen," sometimes these Latvians alone helped consolidate communist control over Russia.

Meanwhile, with 70% of Courland governorate's Latvians gone from the province after 1915, the Latvian nation faced grim prospects if Germany won the war. Unlike in medieval Europe, German peasants of the 20th century now willingly traveled by sea, so that a political "land barrier" like Lithuania of the 1300s would not stop them from settling Courland this time. Nonetheless, because of the Russians' scorched earth tactics, in the winter of 1915-1916, the German army had no choice but to distribute famine relief to the occupied province. Despite this 'humanitarian' action, Courland's military occupation still plundered 20,000,000 marks for Germany (Andersons, 1967, pg. 163). German soldiers logged Courland's forests, emptied its warehouses, and stole countless cultural items – furniture, church bells, porcelain, copper ornaments.

When the German army arrived in 1915, the local Baltic German nobles initially welcomed their "liberators" by offering up one-third of their land for German colonization. Even before the war, with so many Latvians having emigrated for cities or Siberia, the estates of Courland had faced annual labor shortages and shrinking profits. But during wartime, when migrant-laborers were impossible to obtain, the Germans resorted to using Russian prisoners of war to help with harvest. Pragmatically then, the German Empire's army saw an annexed Courland as a raw material supplier and future buyer of German products- a "typical colony" (Andersons, 1967, pg. 157).

Because of the average Latvian's indifference to statehood, in October 1915, the Prussian landholder Alfred von Goßler already summarized them as "more interested in material goods than in any national goals" (Andersons, 1967, pg. 161). In his mind, this alone destined them for Germanization. In the era preceding Nazi Germany's racial class systems, the Latvian and Estonian masses were already considered 'perfect candidates' for Germanization, having "received their culture and freedom" [sic] from centuries of German leadership.

Other Germans concealed their prejudices less skillfully, dismissing the idea that Latvians could be educated or assimilated. Whereas von Goßler admired Latvians for their 'Western' orientation, other Germans described the Latvians as "bastardized Germano-Slavs" with "lively temperaments"- a very enduring, hard-working, intelligent, but dangerous people (Andersons, 1967, pg. 157). This group insisted that educated Latvians were dangerous, and that this danger could only be neutralized through restraining them under indentured servitude.

Alfred von Goßler further hypothesized that the remaining Latvians in Courland wouldn't last long against German colonization (for they had "already spilled much blood and because their natural growth was pitiful") (Andersons, 1967, pg. 164). Goßler speculated that after the war, few Latvian refugees would return to Courland to reclaim their properties either. Therefore, the opportunity to colonize Courland was not one to be missed. With only 20 ethnic-Latvian pastors remaining in Courland in 1916, Goßler believed that by importing a few German intellectuals, he could easily assimilate the remaining Latvians in two generations.

Locating German colonists to settle Courland, however, proved more difficult than expected. In the spring of 1916, while the war's front stagnated along the Daugava, only 11 German families arrived in Courland from Volhynia (northwestern Ukraine) to settle abandoned farmsteads. Despite many German officers sanctioning the colonization projects, German civilians themselves protested this action back home. In the Reichstag, for instance, the liberal Dr. Hugo Haase opposed annexing the Baltic against the inhabitants' will; he declared that Latvians and Estonians had the same right to self-determination as others, a direct nod to American President Wilson's Fourteen Points.[55]

After the disastrous Christmas Battles, however, riots in Petrograd convinced the military to cease supporting the tsar, forcing him to abdicate. With the tsar deposed, many of Russia's minorities felt liberated to agitate for full independence... except for Latvians. While 40,000 Estonian soldiers in Petrograd rallied for Estonian autonomy, the Latvian Riflemen waved a few red-white-red Latvian banners but did little else.

---

55. The Entente's concept of self-determination was intended only for the ethnic minorities of the enemy— Germany, Austria Hungary, and the Ottoman Empire. Self-determination was meant to weaken these empires internally, and didn't apply to Russia's minorities, Britain's colonies, or the United States (Andersons, 1967, pg. 316).

Only in July 1917 did the Latvians finally obtain limited autonomy in Russia. But by this time, a whole row of Latvian political parties had germinated, each promising to dismantle Baltic German supremacy but unwilling to collaborate with another to achieve it. Like the Latvians in that infernal kettle, these parties denounced one another while espousing their own "unique" political formulae. As such, the largest and best-organized Latvian political party remained the Social Democrats, who insisted that even allowing Courland's refugees to return and recover old property would "betray the revolution."[56]

In August of 1917, the most radical Latvian Social Democrats became the Latvian "Bolsheviks" and established the "Iskolats" government in Latvia under the interim government from Petrograd. Iskolats claimed to represent all the workers councils ("soviets") of soldiers and landless peasants within the Latvian-speaking territories. When the Bolshevik coup overthrew the interim government, then in the fall of 1917, Latvians finally tasted the realities of Bolshevism, dispelling their original longing for a messianic and communist "paradise."

Five days after the Bolsheviks coup in Petrograd, the Latvian Bolsheviks declared "Soviet" hegemony over Latvia. Imprisoning opponents and curtailing the press, a Constitutional gathering convened in November for an election. From the election, the Bolsheviks won 72% of the vote, while the Mensheviks (moderate Social Democrats) gained only 5% (Andersons, 1967, pg. 250).

However, the Bolsheviks didn't win Latvia through intimidation alone. Many Latvians voted for the Bolsheviks out of sheer

---

56. E. Andersons quotes the Latvian Bolsheviks: "The proletariat will till Latvia's fields and cultivate its crops, whether they speak German, Russian, or Polish. The proletariat has no ownership of a homeland" (Andersons, 1967, pg. 184).

receptiveness to radical platforms, the charismatic, Bolshevik agenda, and their own hopelessness. As mentioned before, with one of the highest literacy rates in the empire, Latvians had the greatest familiarity with Marxist texts. Furthermore, all Latvian opponents of Bolshevism remained too divided to unite in opposition and escape the 'boiling kettle' together.

In the late fall of 1917, after seizing the popular mandate, the Latvian Bolsheviks began their first Terror. While promising to abolish the nobility's privileges, nationalize the estates, and guarantee social welfare with eight-hour workdays, in December of 1917, the Bolsheviks simply stole everything from everyone. The high productivity of large plantations over small farmstead convinced Iskolats to nationalize the land rather than extending it to landless Latvians. Through Marxist doctrine, the Bolsheviks now viewed the peasants as just another long-term renter who fulfilled obligations in accordance with a centralized, command economy. Thus, communism in Latvia presented only a return to serfdom.

Without profit, Latvians had no incentive to work, and only terror could uphold a system such as this. Demoralized Bolshevik soldiers resorted to banditry, burglarizing schoolhouses and offices or torturing Latvian inhabitants until they revealed hidden grocery caches. The soldiers burned these houses after looting them and shot eyewitnesses anyway: "The Latvian Bolshevik leadership was unable to control their beastly deserters, who lived and looted in the name of Revolution" (Andersons, 1967, pg. 251).

In Petrograd meanwhile, the Bolshevik government abolished all existing legal institutions and founded a "commission against counterrevolution and sabotage"— the Cheka. From its very inception, many Latvians assumed prominence in the Soviet secret police. In his memoirs, the Latvian Mārtiņš Lācis (deputy chief of the Cheka's Terror in Ukraine) openly acknowledged the Cheka's intention to 'exterminate' entire social classes.

With the Bolsheviks in control of Petrograd and acting on Russia's behalf internationally, Germany nonetheless urged them to also realize their long-propagandized line of "ending the war." The Germans offered a truce, the Treaty of Brest-Litovsk, whereby Russia would cede its western agriculture and industry to the Central Powers. Lenin, who the Germans had deliberately transported back to Russia from exile in a sealed train, accepted these demands. To preserve Soviet institutions, Lenin insisted, it was worth sacrificing useful ports (namely, those in Latvia and Estonia) which could be recovered after the Global Revolution anyway.

Leon Trotsky, the Bolshevik Commissar of Foreign Affairs, disagreed. In February 1918, certain that the Central Powers themselves were so overextended as to be almost collapsing themselves, he announced that "there would be neither war, nor peace" (Andersons, 1967, pg. 266). So, when the Bolsheviks stalled in replying to the truce, the German Army pressed further into Russia, capturing the remaining Baltic beyond Riga, Belarus, Crimea, and the Caucasus. In eastern Latvia, the German Army imprisoned everyone associated with Iskolats, Bolshevism, and the 1905 revolution.

In March of 1918, the Bolsheviks now accepted an even harsher version of the original treaty, ceding Finland and Ukraine to the Central Powers. This revised treaty was also far harsher than the conditions imposed on Weimar Germany after the Armistice, long blamed for the "rise of Nazism." Under the new treaty, the Bolsheviks lost 34% of the former empire's population, 85% of its industry, and

90% of its coal reserves (Andersons, 1967, pg. 270). The Central Powers recognized an independent Ukraine, guaranteeing its autonomy but reserving its economic dependence on them. Under the truce, the Baltic German nobles planned to establish a client monarchy (the "United Baltic Duchy") in modern Latvia and Estonia, whereby they could finally realize their colonial dreams.

Despite many of the Russian Empire's anti-Bolshevik minorities living in the territories to be ceded, nonetheless, Bolshevik power was not consolidated across ethnically Russian territories either. To preserve and expand Bolshevik authority, Lenin ordered the Latvian Riflemen to mobilize to the Soviet Union. Promoting them to the role of his personal bodyguards, Lenin projected the image of the Latvians as Soviet Russia's "northern star" for the proletariat (Andersons, 1967, pg. 259). Lenin did not trust ethnic Russian soldiers, who often deserted during dangerous battles and still nursed tsarist sympathies.

After the Communist Revolution, Lenin moved the Soviet Union's capital back to Moscow, Russia's historic capital, to protect the USSR from future foreign incursions. During Moscow's anti-Bolshevik uprisings of 1918, the Latvians in the Cheka alone destroyed many enemies of the Bolsheviks. In late 1919, the Latvian Riflemen struck another fatal blow to Soviet opposition, this time defeating Anton Denikin's "Ukrainian and South Russian" army. Finally, in late 1920, the Latvian "Red" Riflemen fully consolidated Communist control over Ukraine[57] with their successful "Siege of Perekop" in Crimea.

---

57. They say that because of Ukraine's fantastically fertile soils, "Russia without Ukraine is a country, but Russia with Ukraine is an empire."

The 1919 War of Independence

In Europe, German manpower was spread too thin across the Eastern Front to enforce the Treaty of Brest-Litovsk despite its ratification. In the absence of serious German authority, Ukraine had declared independence in November of 1917, followed by Finland in December. Estonia and Lithuania followed in February of 1918, after which came Belarus in March, and Georgia, Armenia, and Azerbaijan in May. Of all Russia's immediate, European neighbors, only the Latvians had not unified or declared independence (Andersons, 1967, pg. 298).

During the summer of 1918, Latvians were either too divided, exiled, or politically apathetic to do so. In 1918, when 225,000 Latvian refugees returned from home exile in Russia, basic survival took precedence over politics (Andersons, 1967, pg. 279). Perturbed by the chaos of a Bolshevik Russia meanwhile, the Latvians sympathetic to Baltic Germans welcomed incorporation into the German Reich or cultural assimilation in the United Baltic Duchy. A German publicist quoted one conservative Latvian as saying: "We can either drink the German's clean water or suffocate in the Russian swamp" (Andersons, 1967, pg. 237).

Nonetheless, the Iskolats Terror in the winter of 1917-1918 had smothered much of the Latvian enthusiasm for communism. At this time, the moderate Latvian Social Democrats voted to divorce from the Bolsheviks, and a nationalist block of Latvians began floating the idea of statehood to everyday Latvians during agricultural seminars. A graduate of the University of Nebraska, the future Latvian president Ulmanis interjected his lectures on swine husbandry with data about how an "independent" Latvia's agricultural productivity compared to that of Switzerland, Belgium, or Denmark. In doing so, he hoped to propose the Latvian state's feasibility to his audience.

During the summer of 1918, Latvia's Baltic Germans themselves became disenchanted with the German military occupation. Despite their initial enthusiasm in 1915, the luster of the Second Reich faded when the German Army collected taxes proportional to assets and income of all Courland's inhabitants. Gone were the days of incompetent or corrupt Russian Imperial tax collectors. After decades of tax evasion, the Baltic German nobles were infuriated that they should suddenly have to pay their fair share.

Furthermore, once the Baltic German barons learned about the poverty and radical politics of the Volga Germans, their excitement for colonization abated further; they suggested accepting only "real" Reich Germans as colonists, from good conservative stock. Unfortunately, the Baltic's instability rarely appealed to any "true" Prussians. Unable to realize their colonial dreams, the Baltic Germans had to tolerate Volhynia's pauperized German liberals in the meantime.

Notwithstanding that Estonia had already declared independence in February, the Baltic Germans proclaimed a United Baltic Duchy ("Baltenlande") in November 1918, including all of Estonia's territory within it. Just days before the Baltic Germans founded the Duchy, German sailors had already raised revolutionary flags on German battleships, and the Kaiser had fled to Holland. During the Duchy's self-proclamation then, the German Empire's former representative to the Baltic, August Winnig, gasped at the Baltic landtag's "absolute lack of insight" into reality; their naivety particularly struck him when they voted to nominate the Second Reich, a country which no longer existed, as their protector.

Thus, while the Bolsheviks remained unable to govern, much less administrate Latvia, the Reichstag in Germany rejected Baltic integration and any further colonization projects there. Both empires abutting Latvia collapsed in 1918, providing the conditions to allow an independent, Latvian state. As future president Ulmanis wrote: "We have a right to our own state. If we want to achieve it, then we will, and no devil can ever take it from us. We can achieve our dreams with our will, our work, and our courage" (Andersons, 1967, pg. 241).

On November 18, 1918, during the German military's curfew, nationalist Latvians and moderate Social Democrats gathered in Riga to proclaim the Republic of Latvia. They invited neither Latvia's wealthiest and most internationally connected inhabitants, the Baltic Germans, nor the Latvian "masses," the Bolsheviks, knowing that both groups would derail their movement.

In the darkness of November 1918, during the 16-hour military curfew in Riga, the Latvian state came into being. Nonetheless, the government held virtually no legitimacy with everyday Latvians. Many believed this government claiming to represent them was too insignificant to make the radical reforms possible. Others were just too apathetic—World War I had scattered one-third of Latvia's inhabitants across the Eurasian steppe, separated families for life, and destroyed 98% of buildings in Latvia along the Daugava River (Andersons, 1967, pg. 585). That a nation the size of West Virginia with just two million people could survive, bordering Russia and Germany, required an exceptional self-confidence bordering on lunacy.[58]

58. This Latvian self-doubt discounted the Estonians, who numbered only 70% of the Latvian population, yet secured their independence with their own military in 1918 and helped to secure Latvia's in 1919.

The success of Latvian republic's government, therefore, hinged on its message of social justice. Ulmanis believed that Latvians could resist Bolshevism so long as every peasant owned land and a means of making income. He knew that communist revolutions did not occur without cause, and that the root problem had to be addressed for the perennial revolts to extinguish. Finally, Ulmanis had the self-confidence to reject the possibility of German victory, to trust in the support of the French and English in the meantime, and to arm every Latvian farmer with weapons should either of these options fail.

While a few Baltic Germans eventually joined the Latvian provisional government, most still feared losing their status and privileges too much to abandon the United Baltic Duchy's idea. By offering the German army one-third of their noble estates for colonization in 1915, they had already set a dangerous precedent for agrarian reform (Andersons, 1967, pg. 357). Rather than betting on and contributing to an independent Latvian state then, many Baltic Germans fought their "weakest" concurrent – the Latvian national government. They hoped for a return to tsarist Russia to protect them from an even more dangerous enemy – the communists.

In December of 1918, just two weeks after Latvia declared independence, the Bolsheviks returned to Latvia. Lenin had sent his soldiers most familiar with the territory, the Latvian Red Riflemen, to incorporate it into the Soviet Union. Through his invasion, Lenin hoped to physically link the Soviet Union with Germany, to which he could then spread the contagion of communism for Global Revolution.

When the Bolsheviks entered Latvia, Ulmanis tried to negotiate with the German army for protection, as thousands of their troops remained in Latvia. When August Winnig counter-offered by demanding citizenship and land for all his German soldiers in Latvia, Ulmanis broke off negotiations. In January, the Bolsheviks captured Riga. Ulmanis sheltered, meanwhile, aboard a battleship on Latvia's western coast.

As the Bolsheviks recaptured nearly all of Latvia's territory in January 1919, they instituted a terror even crueler than Iskolats had in 1917. Famine had overtaken Latvia during that winter of 1918-1919, and when distributing rations,[59] the Bolsheviks divided their "classless society" into three groups of merit. They sentenced the bourgeoise to hard labor packaging war supplies, digging, and hauling bricks or planks. Compensation was not mentioned, and while this labor was not directly a death sentence, "people not conditioned to such hard work cannot survive on the most meager rations" (Aizsilnieks, 1968, pg. 88).

In February, the Bolsheviks next dictated how much clothing anyone could own. By March, they had outlawed inheritances, exempting only the poorest comrades from repurposing the deceased kin's belongings. Latvian author, Ivande Kaija, described the experience:

"Already one and a half months we'd lived in the Bolshevik paradise, and life had drained us beyond telling. Whenever one entered the city, the streets appeared empty like after a plague. Everything was so quiet without pedestrians on the sidewalks—almost all the shops were closed, and the few that were open had nothing to sell on the shelves. That's our paradise. We yearned again

59. Latvian writer Ivande Kaija described the rations, complaining of "worms" in the soup from one kitchen, but perfectly edible broth for a few "missing" their ration cards at another. To resolve the food short- age, fish heads and other entrails became fish "flour." Elsewhere, sticklebacks were netted and boiled into a thick, black 'marmalade' packed into barrels and sent to factories to make oil.

for the 'bourgeoise hell;' in Riga, there was only famine, cold, and illness- a hundred died a day of typhus" (Aizsilnieks, 1968, pg. 100).

Naturally, the stores were empty because the shopkeepers had sold their wares on the black market for three times their state-dictated value. Threats of corporal punishment and execution failed to stamp out this speculation and resource hoarding. Only a continued shortage of groceries in March finally prompted the Bolsheviks to quietly let Latvian farmers into Riga to sell their produce. In May, when Riga's city council elections failed to install a single communist, the Bolsheviks annulled the results.

As the Bolsheviks controlled almost all of Latvia's territory in early 1919, the "Latvian national army" consisted of some 400 "Forest Brothers" holding out in Courland. While Latvia fell almost overnight to the 1919 Bolshevik invasion, the unified and better-organized Estonians had repelled the Bolsheviks at their own border. By the time that Riga fell in January, the Estonian army had already mobilized 74,500 soldiers, 102 artillery batteries, and a handful of armed trains and vehicles. Later, over 100,000 more Estonian reservists joined (Andersons, 1967, pg. 444).

After the Estonians struck down six regiments of Latvian Red Riflemen in Valka, a mixed Latvian-Estonian border town, the Latvian national government signed a mutual aid pact with Estonia. As the Estonians cleared the Bolsheviks from most of northern Latvia's territory, the Latvians compensated them with groceries and materials for Estonian-dictated prices.

Estonia's success, meanwhile, disturbed the Latvian Bolsheviks. According to Marxist theory, the Estonian farmers and workers ought to have spontaneously revolted against their bourgeoise government by now. According to Marxist theory, the working class had no nationality. As such, Estonia's success proved that national loyalties are often stronger than class ones.

In the spring of 1919, the Latvians and Baltic Germans began a counter-offensive from the west, while the Estonians captured Livonia province from the Bolsheviks. Only Latgale, the easternmost province with a Catholic majority and a funny dialect, remained under Bolshevik control. In 1919, Baltic nobles recruited young soldiers from Germany to fight the "Asiatic anti-culture" of Bolshevism, just as bishops had done seven centuries before against the Baltic pagans and Orthodox. Other men in Germany joined the Baltic Germans, viewing Latvia as "free land" for anyone willing to seize it.

1919's Baltic German forces contained many criminal elements outcast from German society, alongside shell-shocked Germans unable to reintegrate as civilians. These criminal elements were present in the Livonian Order of the 1200's as well, when they actively kidnapped and ransomed many of Riga's archbishops. Thus, in 1919, beside the idealistic "patriots" fulfilling Germany's 'historical mission' to the East, the Germans fighters contained other young men seeking good mercenary wages, an adventure, and free land.

The general commanding these men was Rüdiger von der Goltz. Until the Armistice, Von der Goltz represented German interests in Finland, leading the resistance against the Bolsheviks there during the Finnish Civil War. Nonetheless, the Armistice humiliated Von der Goltz's German nationalism, and he scorned the democratic Weimar government as "illegitimate" and "treasonous". Von der Goltz had few friends, but many enemies;[60] when the Latvians saluted the first

60. The Bolsheviks, the Entente, Weimar Germany, and the Latvian Republic's government.

American ships delivering aid, for instance, Von der Goltz remarked wanting to "knock the teeth out" of those "subservient" Latvians (Andersons, 1967, pg. 398).

In April 1919, when the Entente ordered German troops to leave Latvia as part of German disarmament, Von der Goltz organized a coup against the Latvian provisional government instead. Ulmanis escaped prison by sheltering again on the battleship Saratov. In Ulmanis' stead, Von der Goltz installed the Latvian Lutheran minister, Andrievs Niedra[61], to command the Latvian national "government". Von der Goltz recaptured Riga in May from the Bolsheviks and began his monarchist "White Purge" to clear the city of communists.

After completing the purge, Von der Goltz pitted the Latvians against their northern neighbors, the Estonians. He fabricated stories that the Estonians were looting Latvian farmsteads, hoping to divide and conquer as German crusaders did seven centuries before as in Lāčplēsis. Von der Goltz ordered his German troops toward Estonia to topple the national government. Had Von der Goltz succeeded, he would have solidified the nobility's dominance of the Baltic, kept the peasant masses landless, and perpetuated Baltic German supremacy.[62]

The Estonian military engaged the Germans in Cēsis, Latvia, my grandmother's hometown, on the summer solstice of 1919. With Von der Goltz' forces composed of so many mercenaries and German leftovers wanting to go home, they surrendered readily. "Even in the middle of a battle, a mercenary battery sometimes stopped

---

61. Pastor Niedra served the Baltic Germans in 1919 like the traitor "Kangars" did in Lāčplēsis. Kangars is a Latvian witch doctor who betrays Lāčplēsis, revealing to the Black Knight that the hero's superhuman strength in his bear's ears. With this knowledge, the Knight disables Lāčplēsis before pulling him into the Daugava.
62. At least, until the next civil war in the Baltic.

fighting because 'their contract had expired'" (Andersons, 1967, pg. 465). The Estonians captured this abandoned artillery, heavy autos, and wagons of war goods, gladly replenishing their stocks.

Ulmanis, meanwhile, returned to the mainland and reestablished the Latvian provisional government, including two Germans and one Jew in his cabinet. Von der Goltz, despite his defeat, announced in July 1919 that he still wouldn't recognize any Latvian government, or not at least until it proved its dedication to defending Baltic German interests. The Western Entente, fed up with Von der Goltz and his disregard for disarmament, demanded once again he and his Freikorps vacate Latvia.

Unwilling to surrender completely, Von der Goltz transferred his forces to the warlord Pavel Bermondt-Avalov, who rebranded them as the "West Russian Volunteer Army." Bermondt arrived in Latvia in June with many more fighters he'd recruited in Germany using the same promises of land that Von der Goltz had given out. On July 27, 10,000 additional German soldiers took an oath not to leave Latvia until receiving "their" land (Andersons, 1967, pg. 512). Meanwhile, on July 30, Bermondt invited the Latvians to join his forces in restoring order to "their" country.

Nonetheless, the Bermondt's army never intended to grant Latvians equal rights, but to uphold Baltic German supremacy forever. The organization printed its own currency, raided Latvian farmsteads, and demolished the Latvian army's command centers wherever able. In October, Bermondt declared himself Prince Avalov as he pretended to the Russian throne. That October, Bermondt also coordinated with Baltic German nobles and Von der Goltz to attack Riga directly and topple the Latvian and Estonian governments once and for all.

Shortly before attacking Riga, Bermondt spread rumors amongst his soldiers that Latvia was run by "communists" (meaning Ulmanis and the Latvian government) and that the inhabitants of Latvia were "all illiterate"[63] (Andersons, 1967, pg. 522). Abroad, Bermondt's agents circulated stories that the Ulmanis government was cooperating fully. On October 8th, Bermondt's troops attacked Riga. Although Bermondt commanded 40,000 soldiers, he nonetheless requested they pause their assault after fighting for 36 hours in the rain without rest or success.

Skirmishing with Bermondt's army for the next month, the Latvian National army swelled into a 75 000-man fighting force. On November 3, they began a counter-offensive with support from an Estonian armored train and British ammunition. Seeking to maintain the Armistice, the Entente blockaded Germany to force their recall of the German army' s remnants home by November 11, 1919. While Von der Goltz and Bermondt told their forces to disregard this order, many German soldiers declined to sacrifice themselves further for a few adventurists in already hostile territory.

After one final Latvian offensive on the night of November 10th, the Latvians forced Riga's bridges on the morning of the 11th. They liberated the city on what is celebrated today in Latvia as "Lāčplēsis Day." The West Russian Volunteer Army fled back to Germany. As they retreated, the testosterone driven soldiers vandalized Latvian and Lithuanian property along the way.

Ernst von Salomon, a 17-year-old soldier in Von der Goltz' FreiKorps, described the retreat: "We hunted Latvians like rabbits, burned their houses, destroyed their bridges... We threw Latvian

---

63. Latvians were among Russia's most literate ethnicities.

peasants down wells with hand grenades. We destroyed anyone who fell into our hands and set fire to anything that was flammable. As we lost our humanity, we saw everything in a red light… The smoke from our pathway waved like a great, gray flag as our honor and pride smoldered. We left [Latvia] carrying the weight of whatever we looted, leaving nothing for the Latvian" (Andersons, 1967, pg. 536).

Crossing the border into Germany, the Freikorps demonstratively still waved the German imperial and West Russian Volunteer Army flags. One German officer wrote in his memoirs: "We, the German people, know only how to conquer and steal, and our greatest talent is to make others hate us" (Andersons, 1967, pg. 537). After all of his failure in the Baltic, meanwhile, Von der Goltz still insisted on marching to Berlin to overturn the Weimar government. Nobody supported him.[64]

---

64. While many teenaged, German soldiers returned to civilian life after the "Bermondt Affair", others like Ernst von Salomon continued to subsist on hatred for the post-war order. Many in Bermondt's army joined the Nazis a decade later, and Von der Goltz himself joined the Harzburg Front, an anti-democratic, right-wing political alliance in the early 1930's. Many Baltic Germans, like Alfred Rosenberg from northern Estonia, even became involved in the upper echelons of the Nazi Party.

The Agrarian Reform of 1920

After defending Riga and driving out the Bermondtian Army in late 1919, the Latvians designated November 11 a national holiday – "Lāčplēsis Day." Just as in the national myth, when Lāčplēsis resurrects a sunken castle from the depths of Lake Burtnieks, Latvians had finally restored their Castle of Light (Gaismas Pils), their Latvian statehood. Nonetheless, without a meaningful reform to dismantle Latvian exclusion from property ownership, the Latvian state could never secure legitimacy with the people. Only the 1920 Agrarian Reform, facilitated by the Bermondtian retreat,[65] dismantled Baltic German supremacy in Latvia once and for all.

After driving the last Bolsheviks out of eastern Latvia in January 1920, the Latvian state began this reform. Insisting that every Latvian who wanted "his own little corner" could have it ("savs kaktiņš, savs stūrītis zemes"), by the end of 1920, the Latvian government nationalized 2.8 million hectares of land, an area the size of Belgium (Andersons, 1982, pg. 374). This so-called "Land Bank" offered farmsteads both to landless peasants and to tenants with holdings too small to be self-sufficient. Furthermore, the Latvian government distributed these parcels no larger than 22 hectares (54 acres) and prohibited owning anything larger by law to prevent land inequality (Aizsilnieks, 1968, pg. 239).

In 1920, the Latvian government also replaced the currency in use since tsarist time, the ruble, with the "Lats". Valuing each ruble at only 1.3-1.9% of the Lats, the currency exchanged rendered all pre-

---

65. By the end of 1920, half of Latvia's estates were nationalized 'with- out resistance'. The reason for this was that half of Latvia's noble estates were suddenly 'missing' their owners when the Bermondtians retreated. Indeed, while the percentage of Latvians in Latvia between 1914-1920 jumped from 63% to 72%, the German population decreased from 6.1% to 3.6% (a loss of 100 000 people).

war loans and mortgages nearly worthless and erased the pre-war debts of many Latvians (Aizsilnieks, 1968, pg. 182). If before the war, Latvians owed 610 million rubles of mortgage debt (166 rubles for every hectare of land), then after 1920, the population owed only 10 million lats, or 2.7 lats per hectare (Aizsilnieks, 1968, pg. 252). The government anchored this currency to reserves in the National Metal and Chemical Bank in London.

Finally, the Agrarian Reform erased even the little remaining mortgage debt, now valued in Lats. To do this, the Latvian state nationalized all loans extended by Baltic German credit unions and cancelled them, refusing to compensate the nobles for their lost credit. Livonia's Baltic German credit union, hoping to recoup at least some of its lost financial clout, offered the debt-burdened Latvian state a loan to assist with its colossal war debt— 123 million Lats owed to the Western Powers (Andersons, 1967, pg. 584). Unwilling, however, to become beholden to Baltic Germans once again, the Latvian state instead liquidated both Courland's and Livonia's credit unions instead when it nationalized their remaining capital.[66]

While this 'debt nationalization' sounded alarm bell for Western capitalists, the future Latvian Prime Minister, Ādolfs Bļodnieks, wrote: "The new devaluation is certainly unjust against those with savings, but it is equitable for 95% of the population, who finally have the chance to buy their homes and escape from debt" (Aizsilnieks, 1968, pg. 184). Indeed, Latvian peasants, once excluded from owning the very land they'd cultivated since the Great Northern War, could finally build generational wealth. Unfortunately for the wealthiest

---

66. Nationalizing the noble credit unions intended more to liquidate the Latvian government's competitors in the mortgage market rather than to appropriate their capital to cover any war debts (Aizsilnieks, 1968, pg. 253). Only a government mortgage monopoly could fulfill the Agrarian Reform by ensuring equitable redistribution and standardized, universal property sizes.

Latvians, the Agrarian Reform necessarily extinguished the value of government bonds these wealthy patriots had purchased in ruble. This indicates that the Agrarian Reform did not target by ethnicity, but only targeted those with extravagant wealth and privilege.

After transitioning to the Lats, the Latvian government distributed land from the Land Bank to peasants in 22 ha farmstead parcels and nothing greater. This 'optimal' farmstead size was unfortunately not data-based, but simply considered what one family (or "two horses") should need to subsist on. Between 1919-1922, the government extended 31,000 farmsteads, or 60% percent of all new properties created during the Agrarian Reform (Aizsilnieks, 1968, pg. 343). Fighters for Latvia's independence got first pick in the land redistribution, although some of the war-disabled were unable to farm their properties afterward. To the rest of the Latvian peasants, the government advertised land for "10 Lats" a hectare and sold the most fertile farmland for 20 Lats "on credit."

To prevent future monopolies from ever metastasizing back into the state, the government formed the only legal monopolies in the republic: the Land Bank's mortgage monopoly, the forest monopoly "Valsts Mežs,"[67] a linen monopoly, and a liquor monopoly. Despite government mismanagement wasting tremendous profits from these monopolies, historian Aizsilnieks writes about the First Latvian Republic: "It is not enough to have only "good markets," "labor surplus," and "accessible credit or capital," but also the incentive to work and earn something only obtainable after the Agrarian Reform" (Aizsilnieks, 1968, pg. 236). Indeed, by 1928, 230,000 additional Latvian refugees had returned from Russia since

67. In 1921, 84% of Latvian forest belonged to the government. Even in 1937, the state still held 52,4% of the total republic's area, 40,5% of which was forest (Aizsilnieks, 1968, pg. 240).

1918, after they saw the prosperous conditions offered back home (Andersons, 1967, pg. 584). This marked the first time in generations that Latvians returned to Latvia rather than emigrate from it.

With such radical, leftist sentiments pervading Latvian society since the New Current generation, it is not surprising that the 1920 Agrarian Reform was also so radical. Latvia's parliament rejected compensating the formerly landed nobility for the nationalization, voting only to leave them 50 hectares per family. By contrast, Estonia's Agrarian Reform compensated its nobility with 13 million kroons for their lost properties only worth 6 million kroons to begin with (Andersons, 1982, pg. 374).

Incensed with Latvia's disrespect toward private property, in 1924, the Baltic German politician Wilhelm von Fircks announced a lawsuit against Latvia for the Agrarian Reform of 1920. When the Latvian government dismissed Fircks, Latvia received a written copy of the lawsuit sent in 1925 to the League of Nations. This lawsuit presented the next serious challenge between Latvia and the capitalist West. In it, the League would deliberate between national self-determination and protecting the West's most sacred right – private property. The League would also debate as to how far minority rights extended, such as when a formerly privileged class lost their status during another nation's self-determination.

The League notified Latvia it had just two months to defend the Agrarian Reform, or else the suit would move to the International Court of Justice at the Hague. In November of 1925, the Latvian government presented its defense. Their first justification began with a historical motive: in medieval times [sic], the Baltic Germans had stolen the Latvian nation's inheritance and property – its land. Indeed, Baltic Germans from Garlieb Merkel to Rozen had promoted this narrative of seven centuries' enslavement to explain this privileged position. Regardless, the argument did not account for the properties in Latvia that ethnic Russians and other tsarist aristocrats obtained after Tsar Peter.

Latvia's second justification for the Agrarian Reform centered around its national security. Latvian statesmen pointed out that without the reform, the Baltic German estates would have become colonization centers, since the Bermondtian army incentivized many Germans soldiers with land in exchange for mercenary services. "With the help of the nobility of Courland, the Germans wanted to find compensation in the East for what they had lost in the West" (Aizsilnieks, 1968, pg. 234). Thus, the Latvians' impulse for self-preservation drove them toward a sweeping, radical reform.

The third Latvian justification for the Agrarian Reform was socio-political. Those landless peasants, dissatisfied by the ethno- class hierarchy existing for seven centuries (or really just since the Great Northern War) gazed longingly to Bolshevism for justice. Without a means to sustain themselves or sometimes enough bread to eat, "had the Latvian Republic not confiscated and redistributed the estates through the Agrarian Reform, internal unrest would have toppled it" (Aizsilnieks, 1968, pg. 235). Indeed, the battle between capitalists and communists in Latvia, between conservatives and liberals, between those with food and those without it, would have certainly devolved into civil war, just as it had in Russia after 1917.

Finally, the Latvians defended their Agrarian Reform with motives of economic recovery. With Latvia's industry and labor force completely evacuated to Russia in 1915, and with a countryside so ruined that many Latvians inhabited leftover bunkers and trenches, Latvia needed to rebuild. Hunger was as perennial again as in Garlieb Merkel's time; in

1920, Latvia's rye harvest was only half its pre-war crop (Aizsilnieks, 1968, pg. 236). Therefore, the Agrarian Reform functioned to motivate private farmers to rebuild the nation and resume trading with the capitalist Europe.

After receiving these justifications, the League of Nations dithered in its ruling. Their choice pitted the rights to national self-determination and social welfare against the capitalist's sacred right to private property. When Latvian moral and judicial arguments didn't convince the League, however, the Latvians turned to a threat; Latvia's government warned that by overturning the Agrarian Reform, the ensuing unrest would only welcome the Bolsheviks back one step closer to Europe.

On June 8, 1926, the League of Nations "discovered" that Latvia's Agrarian Reform hadn't infringed on any minority rights after all. By guaranteeing their solidarity with the Latvian peasants, the West could maintain a "sanitary corridor" against communist Russia while defending private property back home. As such, threats to private property worked far better than any 'peaceful means' such as talk of morals, rights, or human life. In March of 1927, the League of Nations categorically ruled again in Latvia's favor.

When deputy Wilhelm von Fircks berated the Latvian parliament again for the Agrarian Reform after his loss, a Latvian deputy pointed out that the reform was directed against a privileged class, not an ethnicity. During the Agrarian Reform, 51 ethnic Latvian landholders lost their holdings beside Baltic Germans, Russians, and Poles.

Although the Agrarian Reform was indeed "rushed", suffered discrepancies, and exposed to corruption, for the first time in Latvian history, it also guaranteed a general social equity to Latvians. The "volcanic rumblings" of peasant unrest, perennial since Garlieb

Merkel wrote Die Letten in the 18th century, had finally quelled. The Agrarian Reform guaranteed Latvians the social stability and prestige to join other world leaders as equals in the League of Nations. A Latvian nation state now protected the Latvian language from the "fate of the backwater" befalling Belarusians, or from experiencing the genocidal famine and cultural erasure that the Ukrainians suffered under Stalin in the 1930's.

As for the fate of the Baltic Germans: In 1796, when Garlieb Merkel forewarned of a terrible conflagration should the Latvian peasant's abuse continue, nobody heeded him. Instead, the Baltic Germans ignored or subverted reform, choosing personal wealth and privilege over their ethnicity's immortality. After the Communist Revolution, the Latvian Agrarian Reform of 1920, the Holocaust, and the expulsion of all Germans east of the Oder in 1945, Eastern Europe today bears little resemblance to what it did in either 1796, 1914, or 1940.

As the modern American figure of social justice, a figure whose legacy white Americans sanitize wherever possible, Martin Luther King Jr, once said: "The arc of the moral universe is long, but it bends toward justice." For two centuries, Latvia's conservative forces refused to address injustice around them, only prolonging the 'caged tiger's' captivity. For their refusal, they paid with their existence. Today, Latvia's current German population numbers 3,000, or even less people than the number of remaining Jewish people in Latvia since the Holocaust.

Works Consulted or Cited

Aizsilnieks, A. (1968). Latvijas Saimniecības Vēsture: 1914-1945. Sundbyberg, Sweden: Daugava.

Andersons, E. (1967). Latvijas Vēsture: 1914-1920. Stockholm, Sweden: Daugava.

Andersons, E. (1982). Latvijas Vēsture: 1920-1940 Ārpolītika I. Stockholm, Sweden: Daugava.

Dearen, J. (2021, December 23). He wore a wire, risked his life to expose who was in the KKK. Retrieved from Associated Press News: https://apnews.com/article/florida-race-and-ethnicity-racial-injustice-veterans-ku-klux-klan-fa0ec4120b1457f56c527108074795b5

Dunsdorfs, E. (1962). Latvijas Vēsture: 1600-1710. Uppsala, Sweden: Daugava.

Dunsdorfs, E. (1964). Latvijas Vēsture: 1500-1600. Stockholm, Sweden: Daugava.

Dunsdorfs, E. (1973). Latvijas Vēsture: 1710-1800. Sundbyberg, Sweden: Daugava.

Ģērmanis, U. (1990). Latviešu Tautas Piedzīvojumi. Jāņa Sēta.

Iedzīvotāju starptautiskā ilgtermiņa migrācija pa valstu grupām 1990 - 2020. (2022, March 10). Retrieved from Latvijas Oficiālās Statistikas Portāla Datubāze: https://data.stat.gov.lv/pxweb/en/OSP_PUB/START__POP__IB__IBE/IBE010/table/tableViewLayout1/

Johansons, A. (1975). Latvijas Kultūras Vēsture: 1710-1800. Stockholm, Sweden: Daugava.

Merķelis, G. (2016). Latvieši ("Die Letten"). Riga, Latvia: Zvaigzne ABC.

Pumpurs, A. (1989). Lāčplēsis. Lincoln, Nebraska: Augstums Printing Service, Inc.

Quarterly Homeownership Rates by Race and Ethnicity of Householder for the United States: 1994-2021. (2021). Retrieved from Us Census Bureau: https://www.census.gov/housing/hvs/data/charts/fig08.pdf

Self-Described Member of "Boogaloo Bois" Charged with Riot. (2020, October 23). Retrieved from United States Department of Justice: https://www.justice.gov/usao-mn/pr/self-described-member-boogaloo-bois-charged-riot

Šterns, I. (1997). Latvijas Vēsture: 1290-1500. Latvia: Daugava.

Švābe, A. (1958). Latvijas Vēsture: 1800-1914. Uppsala, Sweden: Daugava.

Turlajs, J. (2005). Latvijas Vēstures Atlants. Riga: Jāņa Sēta.

Wikimedia Commons. (2022, April 5). Retrieved from https://commons.wikimedia.org/wiki/File:1900sc_Postcard-Alligator_01.jpg

Wikimedia Commons. (2022, April 5). Retrieved from https://commons.wikimedia.org/wiki/File:Scourged_back_by_McPherson_%26_Oliver,_1863,_retouched.jpg

Wikimedia Commons. (2022, April 5). Retrieved from https://commons.wikimedia.org/wiki/File:Latvia_adm_location_map.svg

Wilkerson, I. (2010). The Warmth of Other Suns. New York: Vintage Books.

Wilkerson, I. (2020). Caste - The Origins of Our Discontents. New York: Random House.

Made in the USA
Columbia, SC
06 October 2022

68157858R00108